D0518575

WITHDRAWN FROM STOCK

THE SURREY INSTITUTE OF ART & DESIGN
FARNHAM CAMPUS
01252 722441 x 2249

FINES WILL BE CHARGED ON OVERDUE BOOKS
Return on or before the last date stamped below.

24. JAN 97	2 9 APR 2002		
09. OCT	1 3 DEC 2002		
27. NOV. 1998			
11. DEC. 1998	9 JAN 2004		
15. JAN 1999	1 9 JAN 2005		
1 - OCT 2001			
1 5 APR 2002	1 8 FEB 2005		
1 7 JAN 2003	1 5 SEP 2006		
1 6 OCT 2006	24/10/11		

The Visualization Quest

The Visualization Quest
A History of Computer Animation

Valliere Richard Auzenne

Rutherford • Madison • Teaneck
Fairleigh Dickinson University Press
London and Toronto: Associated University Presses

© 1994 by Associated University Presses, Inc.

All rights reserved. Authorization to photocopy items for internal or personal use, or the internal or personal use of specific clients, is granted by the copyright owner, provided that a base fee of $10.00, plus eight cents per page, per copy is paid directly to the Copyright Clearance Center, 27 Congress Street, Salem, Massachusetts 01970. [0-8386-3440-0/94 $10.00 + 8¢ pp, pc.]

Associated University Presses
440 Forsgate Drive
Cranbury, NJ 08512

Associated University Presses
25 Sicilian Avenue
London WC1A 2QH, England

Associated University Presses
P.O. Box 338, Port Credit
Mississauga, Ontario
Canada L5G 4L8

The paper used in this publication meets the requirements
of the American National Standard for Permanence of Paper
for Printed Library Materials Z39.48-1984.

Library of Congress Cataloging-in-Publication Data

Auzenne, Valliere Richard, 1952
    The visualization quest : a history of computer animation /
Valliere Richard Auzenne.
      p. cm.
    Includes bibliographical references and index.
    ISBN 0-8386-3440-0 (alk. paper)
    1. Computer animation—History.   I. Title.
TR897.5.A9   1994
006.6—dc20   90-56229
                                     CIP

THE LIBRARY
West Surrey College of Art and Design

791.4330285 Auz

PRINTED IN THE UNITED STATES OF AMERICA

Contents

Acknowledgments

I wish to express my sincere appreciation to the many individuals in the computer animation industry who allowed me to interview them and who freely and openly shared information and viewpoints, for without their support, this book would not have been possible.

I am especially indebted to Patric Prince for her support and aid in the identification and location of key individuals and institutions, and for her boundless personal insights and encouragement.

I am deeply grateful to Dr. Marilyn Young, for her guidance, assistance, and endless patience, and to Dean Theodore Clevenger, Dr. Edward Fernald, Dr. Norman Medoff, and Paul Rutkovsky for their invaluable insights, suggestions, and criticisms.

I am also obliged to Dr. Thomas Hoffer for his interest and support in the beginning of this project and to Dr. Bernie Blackman, who designed the qualitative software program "Qualpro," which aided me immensely in organizing the interview materials.

I also wish to thank Karen Johnson and Andrew Harlow for their support and aid in bringing this manuscript to publication.

I would like to express my deepest gratitude to the McKnight Foundation and the Florida Endowment Fund for their generous financial support and to Dr. Israel Tribble, president of the Florida Endowment Funds and my comrade McKnight Fellows for their continual personal support.

In conclusion, I wish to thank my parents, Edward and Valliere Richard, for their love and unceasing confidence in my abilities, and my husband, George R. Auzenne, for his continued support and encouragement.

*　*　*

All illustrations in this volume are reproduced by permission.

The Visualization Quest

THE LIBRARY
West Surrey College of Art and Design

Introduction

Animation is defined as "the bringing of apparent life to inanimate objects" (Mancis & Van Dyke 1966, 100). It is the creation of movement and ultimately the creation of life in film. Since its inception, animation has served as an effective vehicle for communication. Computer animation has the ability to efficaciously convey statements, ideas, theories, and emotions. This is exemplified by the diverse subjects and applications which have been realized through the use of this medium. The newest genre, computer animation, continues the tradition of communicator. It is used widely to illustrate mathematical formulas and molecule structures, to advertise products, to instruct, to make social statements, and to entertain.

Computer animation embraces the major element in animation—it indeed "brings life to inanimate objects" through the varied roles it performs in animation generation. The computer is used to create drawings, movement, and color, as well as to photograph or edit.

The ability to communicate through computer animation is the result of the symbiotic relationship between science and art that exists in this medium. This mutual dependence bonds the creative abilities of two disciplines whose epistemology is rooted in opposing camps. The scientific, adopting a World View I position, the "received view," is based on discovery, and assumes there is a "physical, knowable reality that is self evident" (Littlejohn 1983, p. 25). The artistic, which embraces a World View II stance, is based on interaction and interpretation, and assumes that "people take an active role in creating knowledge" (Littlejohn 1983, p. 25).

In order to discern the function this cooperative has had in the evolution of computer animation, it is necessary to understand how this medium developed, why it advanced in this way, and who was involved in the development.

The Visualization Quest traces the developments of this new communication field, and investigates the unusual alliance between science and art. It also provides a rare and unique look into key issues which influenced and shaped the history of this medium.

The key individuals, companies, and institutions involved in the development of computer animation are identified and individually profiled. These profiles provide insight into the decisions of the individuals who were involved in the development of this new medium and illustrate how these decisions defined the direction of computer animation.

1
Types of Computer Animation

Computer animation is best defined by the function it provides in the creation of animation, for as Thalmann and Thalmann state, "the term 'computer animation' is imprecise and can sometimes be misleading" (Thalmann and Thalmann 1985, 13). The major reason for this confusion is that the term computer animation encompasses a variety of applications which include generation of drawings, movement, and color. Judson Rosebush lists the specific tasks which the computer is capable of performing in the production of computer animation as

> motion graphics, motion control, video synthesizers, image processing, computer assisted cartoon animation, paint systems, special effects, three-dimensional image synthesis simulation and robotics. (1988, 17)

These tasks can be divided into two classifications—computer-assisted, which is also referred to as key-framed animation, and computer-generated animation, also called modeled animation. Key-framed animation is used to aid in the conventional two-dimensional animation stages such as in-betweening and the computation of the movement of two-dimensional objects. Modeled animation is more complex and is used to create three-dimensional images. A third area employs computers in motion control photography, where the computer is used to control the positioning and movement of the camera (Fox and Waite 1984, 118).

Computer-Assisted/Key-Frame Animation

Computer-assisted or key-frame animation consists of six possible functions: the input of drawings, the production of in-betweens, the specification of motion of an object along a path, the coloring of drawings and backgrounds, the synchronization of motion with sound, and the initiation of recording a sequence on film or videotape (Thalmann 1985, 43).

In computer-assisted animation, drawings can be created, modified, and altered, combined with other drawings, or saved and retrieved by a graphics editor. The most useful capability offered, however, is the tedious production of in-betweens (drawings that are between the extreme or key points of movement in an animation [Madsen 1969, 116]). In traditional animation this stage is performed by the assistant animator or in-betweener. However, the computer has the capacity to calculate additional drawings between two key drawings that depict the extreme position or the most expressive characteristics of the motion. Two examples of these types of programs are Nester Burtnyk and Marceli Wein's (developed in 1970) on which Peter Foldes produced his film *Hunger,* and Ed Catmull's program "TWEEN" (which was developed in 1979 at NYIT's Computer Graphics Lab). "TWEEN" was designed to aid the artist in the generation and manipulation of digitally produced images. "At any time the artist can review the in-betweens and modify them with an electronic pen; the computer recalculates the other in-betweens" (Thalmann and Thalmann 1984, 35). Coloring, drawings, and backgrounds are achieved through the use of graphics editors such as Nadia Magnenat-Thalmann's "GRAFEDIT," or paint systems. Richard Shoup's "Superpaint" program, developed at Xerox Palo Alto Research Center (PARC), and Alvy Ray Smith's digital paint program "PAINT," developed at NYIT, are two examples of such paint programs. Smith, in describing his program, stated that

> paint is a menu-driven computer program hand painting two-dimensional images in full color. It is a highly interactive software package with which a human artist may employ the power of a digital computer to compose paintings which are entirely of his own creation. (Smith 1978, 1)

Motion Control

Motion control is defined by James Hahn (1988, 101) as the "specification of position and orientation of objects in time." It is a technique which was introduced by Robert Abel in 1971, in which he used computers to move the camera in order to eliminate human error and time-consuming placement of cameras and objects in complicated scenes. As Fox and Waite describe the process, the camera has several motors that

> can change its position in almost any direction by small increments. The camera may be snapping pictures of a spaceship model, for example, while revolving around the model, giving the illusion that the ship is moving. The computer simplifies the calculations for pans (left to right movements), tilts, rotations, and accelerations. (Fox and Waite 1984, 118)

Modeled/Computer-Generated Animation

Modeled or computer-generated animation is used in the creation of three-dimensional images. "Modeling is the creation of the 3-D database which serves as the 'world' to be portrayed in a synthetic computer graphics sequence" (Smith 1983, 28). Models fall into two basic categories: two-dimensional and three-dimensional. Although the image which appears on the display screen is always two-dimensional, the reference to two-dimensional and three-dimensional graphics applies to the model which is used to *generate* the image, *not* what appears on the display screen or monitor (Jankel and Morton 1984, 30).

Three-dimensional (3-D) animation consists of three principle functions: objective modeling, motion specification, and synchronization and image rendering.

Object modeling, which uses either wire-frame or solid models, involves the description and construction of three-dimensional objects. Wire-framed models, which are the "oldest and simplest," are based specifically on three-dimensional line drawings, and do not possess the capability of creating realistic images. Solid models, on the other hand, are based on two and three-dimensional surfaces and provide more descriptive information, offering the ability to produce a greater degree of realism (Thalmann 1985, 69).

There are three methods used to create wire-frame or solid model objects: digitization, graphics editing, and programming. Digitization is a process where a photograph or a drawing of an object is traced on a grid and then photographed from various angles. The photographs are then digitized using a software program which reconstructs the image in a three-dimensional form (Thalmann 1985,

74). The now-defunct Information International Inc., also known as Triple I, used this technique in the film *Futureworld* (Smith 1983, 31). Graphics editing is a method which employs the use of an interactive tool, the graphics editor, to construct a three-dimensional object by using existing geometric shapes such as cubes, cones, spheres, and cylinders. One example of an interactive, general purpose, three-dimensional graphics editor is Nadia Magnenat-Thalmann's "Body-Building." It offers the ability to

> create three-dimensional objects, to modify them by geometrical transformations, and to assemble them to obtain a complete drawing. The drawing can be stored on file; later, it can be retrieved for further modifications, or a hard copy can be obtained. (Thalmann and Thalmann 1985, 75)

A program is a series of instructions that directs the computer to perform specific operations in a precise order (Wilson 1986, 44). Programming is the process by which these directions are established.

In three-dimensional computer animation the term "motion" conveys several meanings. Thalmann & Thalmann define them as:

1. physical motions like rotations or transformations of an object
2. physical transformations like alterations of the shape, size, or color of an object
3. virtual camera motion. (Thalmann and Thalmann 1985, 77)

Motion specification and synchronization is the defining and timing of these operations in three-dimensional model animation. It is the function which dictates how an image moves, where it moves, and if and how it interacts with other objects.

Image rendering is "the process of using the computer model of an object or scene to create its picture" (Lanthrop 1988, 2). "It is the frame-by-frame realization of the data base into two dimensions" (Smith 1983, 28), and is achieved by the incorporation of shadows, shading, and textures. Two of the most widely used methods of rendering are the depth buffer, or Z buffer, and ray tracing.

Depth buffering, or Z buffering, was developed by Ed Catmull of Pixar, while he was at the University of Utah (Catmull 1974). It is the fastest and most predominant method of rendering solid objects. The only drawback is that it does not do a good job of rendering images with shadows or transparent reflective images (Lanthrop 1988, 8).

Ray tracing, on the other hand, is capable of rendering shadows, reflective and transparent objects. It is the method currently used for maximum image quality. One of the key researchers in this area of computer animation is Jim Kajiya, who is currently at the California Institute of Technology (Kajiya 1983).

These functions, applications, and techniques describe the elements which constitute computer animation and provide a more accurate definition of the medium.

2

Uses of Computer Animation

Computer animation has numerous applications ranging from the visualization of mathematical and scientific data to the simulation of nonexistent environments. It is used in the creation of special effects and simulated characters, and in the solicitation of products and ideas.

As Alyce Kaprow at the 1988 SIGGRAPH conference session "Computer Graphics and the Changing Methodology for Artists and Designers" stated:

> Computers are unique tools. They can emulate the old, they create the new, they synthesize the old and the new with opportunities to reorder.

> We are no longer bound by what we have known always as the real world. We can create our own universe . . . the computer creates new models of our universe from which to explore solutions. The computer allows us to order our universe differently, to unite tools, to give us new ways to solve problems.

> Computers support risk. They allow us the opportunity to create ideas and develop concepts, and to experiment. They store and retrieve and they give us the flexibility to try alternatives and manipulations. (SIG-GRAPH '88 Panel Proceedings, p. 14)

Computer animation is the vehicle providing the computer with the capabilities to which Alyce Kaprow refers. More specifically, *computer animation* is the tool which "supports risk," "creates new models of our universe," and offers the ability to explore alternatives. These capabilities or applications can be categorized into six basic areas: mathematics, science, entertainment, advertising, education, and art.

Mathematical Applications

Computers have been aiding mathematics since their inception by performing complex computations. More recently, through computer

Hypertorous projected in four-dimensional space with cylindrical bands partially removed. Dr. Thomas F. Banchoff.

animation, they not only perform these elaborate calculations, but they produce images which help visualize mathematical concepts. This is a symbiotic relationship, for just as computer animation has contributed to the understanding and development of mathematics, as in the visualization of the Mandelbrot set by Heinz-Otto Peitgen, mathematics has promoted the advancement of computer animation by commanding ingenuity to present four (and more) dimensional images in three-dimensional forms. Some of the areas in which computer animation has been and is utilized to illustrate traditionally unseen mathematical phenomena include Thomas Banchoff's research on hypercubes and hyperspheres and Nelson Max's research in topology.

Thomas Banchoff at Brown University has provided a way for mathematicians to visualize and explore the properties of geometric forms. Banchoff states that "by looking at the pictures we were able to see new relationships and turn those into theorems" (personal interview, 3 August 1988).

Topology "focuses on geometrical features that remain unchanged after twisting, stretching, and other deformations are imposed on a geometric space" (Peterson 1988, 10).

Scientific Applications

The presence of computer animation in scientific fields represents a diverse body of work, but with two focused and related goals—the visualization of data and the fabrication of useful images. Nelson Max's film *Tomato Bushy Stunt Virus* is one example of how such data visualization aids scientific research:

> The first step in combating the virus was to determine where the active sites lay and what they looked like. The structure of the virus was investigated by X-ray crystallography and a data library built up of the information obtained. Nelson Max used this to model the virus on a computer and view it as a realistic assembly of spheres complete with hidden surfaces removed, shading and highlights. The results were displayed using raster graphics techniques and a film was made which demonstrated the structure of the virus. (Jankel and Morton 1984, 69)

This process assisted the scientists in gaining a better understanding of the properties of the virus in order to develop an effective vaccine.

Another scientific application, which is a current joint project between Calvin Chan at the CADRE Institute at San Jose State University, Lisa Johannson of the Orthopedic Biomechanics Laboratory at Shriners Hospital in San Francisco, and Joel Slayton at San Jose State University, is referred to affectionately as "Sophie" or more descriptively as "Hand." Slayton described the project at a panel session at the 1988 SIGGRAPH:

> A company called VPL had developed an interactive glove device that you could wear and connect to a computer. We decided that it would be appropriate to develop a higher resolution model of the human hand that would seem like yours and would allow you to interact with the glove in a more articulated way. So we went about building a cosmetic prosthesis, digitizing it with a three-dimensional digitizer in a fairly specific way, lots of experimentation . . . and finally arriving at a fairly articulated model of the hand. (SIGGRAPH 88, August, Panel Proceedings, 11 & 12)

Slayton acknowledged that there was no specific application which had been identified for the use of "Hand," but that there were many potentials, including the possibility of biomedical purposes.

Indeed, computer animation has many current medical applications. It is used to assist surgery procedure strategies, to illustrate spreading disease patterns, and to aid analysis of physical abnormalities due to medical conditions.

Other scientific applications include the visualization of molecule structures, such as Nelson Max's DNA molecules, or the now-defunct Cranston Csuri's illustrations of body parts and muscles which was used in a television series *The Body Machine.*

Medical and scientific needs continue to challenge computer animation to find new means to aid these fields and assist in the rendering of better medical care.

Entertainment Applications

Entertainment applications in computer animation can be divided into three categories: feature films, advertising, and the emerging shorts (produced mainly to illustrate new uses and new software and hardware developments). These are generally aimed for debut at SIGGRAPH's film and video show. Ed Catmull of Pixar explains how this trend evolved:

> The first film shows had a heavy video content. One of the new trends was that we began to see more and more animation sample reels from companies making commercials.

> Then a new trend emerged, because people were getting tired of commercials. Some companies began producing films that had no commercial value. They were doing little art pieces. Those films tended to be better because there was a competition to do a great little piece. There was an implied competition. (E. Catmull, personal interview, 19 May 1988)

Feature Films

The first film to use computer animation was *Westworld,* which was produced by MGM and released in 1973. Computer animation was used to create the illusion of the visual perception of a robot. The sequel to *Westworld, Futureworld,* which debuted in 1976, as well as *Looker, Star Trek II: The Wrath of Khan* and *TRON* all employed full-color raster graphics (Smith 1983, 28).

TRON still holds the record for the most computer animation used in a feature film. It took the talent and facilities of four companies—MAGI, Information International Inc. (Triple I), Robert Abel and Associates, and Digital Effects. Richard Taylor, who supervised the effects simulation, described the distribution of work in an 1988 interview:

> The three companies that worked on *TRON,* that I supervised doing the effects simulation, were Triple I, MAGI, and Bob Abel who did a few things in a different form, that wasn't raster graphics. I also had Digital Effects in New York do one piece. No one company could have generated the amount of imagery by themselves. (R. Taylor, personal interview, 2 August 1988)

The *Star Trek II*'s Genesis sequence was one of the most creative and challenging projects to employ computer animation. Pixar, then part of Lucasfilm, was approached by Industrial Light and Magic, the special effects section of Lucasfilm, to aid them in the visualization of a genesis effect, "turning death into life," according to Alvy Ray Smith. Loren Carpenter of Pixar recalls:

> This was our first real project—the first time we'd taken all these tools that we'd developed and try to use them for something bigger than a test case. (Personal interview, 22 January 1988)

Several computer animation techniques were used in this 67-second sequence. Bill Reeves used a procedural model for the wall of fire, and Loren Carpenter used fractals for the landscapes.

Independent computer animator Larry Cuba, a protégé of John Whitney, Sr., who also served as his programmer, created the black-and-white computer animation sequence which appeared in *Star Trek I.* It was a "simulation of a computer diagram of the 'Death Star' which the rebel pilots watch during their briefing session" (Perlman 1980, 3). Cuba produced this two-minute sequence on Tom De-Fanti's GRASS system in Chicago.

Advertising Applications

Mathematical Applications Group Inc. (MAGI) was one of the first companies to introduce computer animation to the public via commercials. Phillip Mittelman, founder of MAGI, described in a personal interview their entry into the advertising and commercial field:

> About 1967 we made our first pictures and from then on we were in the graphics field. We went public in 1969. Then we started doing commercial work. We did some television commercials and some logos. The first job that we ever did was in early 1969 for IBM. They had an office products division and they wanted to have a film showing letters flying around as though they were coming out of a word processor. It was black and white. (P. Mittelman, personal interview, 11 May 1988)

The 1980s introduced a new trend, as Margo Wilson noted: "commercials, not movies, have become the prime showcase of [the] computer animator's artistic talents" (Wilson 1986, 24).

In the early 1980s, three companies appeared to dominate the production of computer animation for use in commercials. They were Robert Abel and Associates, Information International Inc. (Triple I), and Digital Productions. All three companies have since gone out of business.

Robert Abel and Associates, although defunct, became a legend for its superbly executed and creative work, termed close to perfection by many. There is speculation that this might have been the reason for its downfall; however, Robert Abel and Associates continues to hold a standard by which others evaluate their work. Examples of the unique quality and creative flavor of Abel's work include the "Brilliance" commercial with the sexy robot, the series of TRW advertisements where images of ancient artifacts lead us to a modern era, and the promotional and opening for Steven Spielberg's television series *Amazing Stories*.

A notable company that emerged during this period, and which now appears to be the only production house to have successfully survived the turbulence of takeovers, is Pacific Data Images (PDI), founded in 1980 by Carl Rosendahl. It has been responsible for many of the network television logos and for the Crest dancing toothpaste commercial.

Information International Inc. (Triple I), after folding as the result of an unfriendly takeover, was the main feeder company for Digital Productions. It was founded by the same two individuals, John Whitney, Jr. and Gary Demos, who established Whitney-Demos, which folded in 1989. Although these individuals failed to establish a lasting enterprise, the visual products of their collaboration consistently incorporate fresh new visual concepts which are rendered exquisitely and exhibit exceptional technical proficiency.

Educational Applications

Educational applications of computer animation encompass a variety of subjects ranging from the illustration of mathematical concepts or physical laws, as in Jim Blinn's *Mechanical Universe,* to the social statements of Peter Foldes in his computer animated film *Hunger.* The use of computer animation as a teaching tool can be divided into two categories: illustration of concepts and ideas, and active participation.

The leading individual in the creation of computer animation for illustrative purposes in education is Jim Blinn of the California Institute of Technology (CalTech). He is responsible for over seven hours worth of computer animation for the educational television college course series *Mechanical Universe.* The course, produced by CalTech in cooperation with the Corporation for Community College Television and funded by the Annenberg/CPB Project, as 52 half-hour episodes and over 530 scenes of computer animation. Blinn is also responsible for producing realisitc animations depicting U.S. space missions to Jupiter, Saturn, Uranus, and Neptune, as well as the international missions to Halley's comet.

Active participation can also be described as interactive capability. One of the leaders in developing this form of computer animation is Tom DeFanti at the University of Illinois, Chicago Campus. DeFanti is responsible for the development of tools such as GRASS, a three-dimensional real-time system which he developed at Ohio State University, and ZGRASS, which he developed after moving to Chicago. These instruments have the ability to aid the artist as well as the scientist in depicting their views of the cultures within the world, be they organisms, individuals, or societies.

In 1973, Tom DeFanti and Dan Sandin established a cooperative computer workspace called the "Circle Graphics Habitat." Sandin described the objectives and goals of the habitat during a 1988 interview:

The goal of the Circle Graphics Habitat was to be able to do low-cost, very fast, graphics. We viewed it as kind of a short-order educational media house.

At that time there was actually quite a bit of interest in using technology in education, especially computer-generated video.

It was the most interactive, easy-to-use arts base I've ever seen. We did educational materials and several video pieces.

We want to set up environments where researchers teach people in industry and other researchers about their research field. (personal interview, 9 February 1988)

Although the Circle Graphics Habitat closed in 1983, the development of interactive equipment and products of those tools continue to be a priority for Tom DeFanti and Dan Sandin. As Sandin stated:

Now there's a tremendous amount of talk about scientific visualization. Again, there is a new increase in the interest in computer-mediated education. (personal interview, 9 February 1988)

An example of Sandin's term "computer-mediated education" is Brown University's computer science department research study of the applications of workstation technology for education and research. It consists of a unique environment which was specially constructed and equipped. Andries van Dam describes his colleague Robert Sedgewick's project:

We inaugurated a novel electronic classroom equipped with 55 high-performance workstations connected in a high-speed network. Most introductory courses in the computer science curriculum are now taught in this specially constructed auditorium, as are courses in differential equations, differential geometry, and neuroscience.

Our aim is to offer students an opportunity to 'see' an abstract phenomenon. (1984, 158)

These are a few examples of the basic uses in which computer animation is employed. Although varied, they share the same common goal, to provide the opportunity to communicate visually.

3

Institutional Roots of Computer Animation

Computer animation's origins lie in seven distinct institutions: three educational (Massachusetts Institute of Technology, University of Utah, Ohio State University); two national research centers (Lawrence Livermore National Laboratory, the Jet Propulsion Laboratory); one private corporation (Boeing); and one utility company (Bell Telephone Laboratories). The developments that occurred at these institutions formed the foundation for what is now called computer graphics and computer animation. In 1960 William Fetter at Boeing designated the term "computer graphics" to

> explain the output of a computer, drawing-machine, and artist combination. . . . Point by point measurements of aircraft were recorded on punch cards. The points formed the basis of connect-the-dots drawings produced on an x-y plotter-verifier, an automatic drafting machine directed by computer tape programmed from the measurements. Extremely accurate drawings resulted and, because the program could run with variations of perspective views, a series of drawings could be made and translated into film animations. (Fetter 1964)

It seems appropriate, in keeping with Fetter's definition of computer graphics, that these "film animations" be referred to as computer animations. There exists not only a strong relationship between computer graphics and computer animation, but mutual roots as well. Therefore, surveying the foundation of computer graphics is also examining the establishment of computer animation.

Boeing

Boeing Company in Seattle was one of the first companies to employ computer graphics and computer animation. An airplane manufacturing company, Boeing's concentration in computer animation

26

centered quite naturally on aircraft design. William Fetter, one of the leading researchers at Boeing, utilized computer graphics in a study on cockpit design (Fetter 1964). As part of the project, Fetter modeled a human figure and became the first individual to model a human via computer. Eugene Youngblood in *Expanded Cinema,* describes Fetter's work:

> William Fetter of the Boeing Company in Seattle has used mechanical analog plotting systems to make animated films for visualizing pilot and cockpit configurations in aircraft design. (1970, 194)

As a result of this research, Fetter began focusing on human figure simulation; he left Boeing in 1969 (Rosebush 1979, 30).

Massachusetts Institute of Technology (Lincoln Laboratory)

The Whirlwind, a mainframe computer, was built at MIT in 1949, and in the early 1950s was fitted with a cathode ray tube display specifically designed for plotting pictures. It consisted of

> the MIT Lincoln Laboratory TX-2 computer, CRT display, light pen, plotter, command buttons, and analog knobs. (Sutherland 1963)

The light pen provided a limited interaction with the displayed picture (Jankel and Morton 1984, 18). With this technology already in place, the stage had been set for the next step in computer graphics, the pursuit of interactive computer graphics and animation by Ivan Sutherland. Interactive graphics as defined by Carl Machover is:

> Graphics operations using a computer graphics display system to allow the operator to create and alter the displayed images in response to commands entered by means of the input devices. (1988, 689-188-10)

Ivan Sutherland is often called the father of interactive computer graphics. His Ph.D. thesis, "Sketchpad: a man-machine graphical communication system" (Sutherland 1963), opened the door to interactive computer graphics and computer animation. Sketchpad was designed so that the user could draw directly on the cathode-ray tube (CRT) with a light pen—a photoelectric cell inside a pen-like device. Any movement of the pen across the monitor was demarcated on the screen by a path of light. (Goodman 1987, 21)

Sutherland also explored Sketchpad's computer animation, capabilities:

He also made a sketch of a girl's face and by successively substituting for an open eye, half, quarter, and fully closed versions, he made her wink. (Machover 1984, 146)

In reaction to Sketchpad's potential to generate animation, Sutherland projected:

The ability to make moving drawings suggests that Sketchpad might be used for making animated cartoons. (Machover 1984, 146)

Another significant event was the establishment of The Center for Advanced Visual Studies at MIT in 1967 by artist and educator Gyorgy Kepes. It has served as a setting and a catalyst for collaborative work between artists and scientists. Computer animator and Bell Laboratories artist resident Stan VanderBeek and experimental animator John Whitney, Sr. were two of the early fellows, along with Otto Piene, who is currently the director of the center.

Bell Laboratories

Edward Zajac made the first computer animated film, *Two-Gyro Gravity-Gradient Attitude Control System,* at Bell Laboratories in 1961 (Thalmann and Thalmann 1985, 221). The wire-frame animated film was a product of a study which Zajac was conducting in order to

determine whether a satellite in space could be stabilized to have one of its sides constantly facing earth. (Goodman 1987, 153)

Zajac found computer animation to be the best method to illustrate his findings.

Following close in his footsteps were Ken Knowlton, Stan VanderBeek, Lillian Schwartz, A. Michael Noll, and Frank Sinden, all at Bell Laboratories.

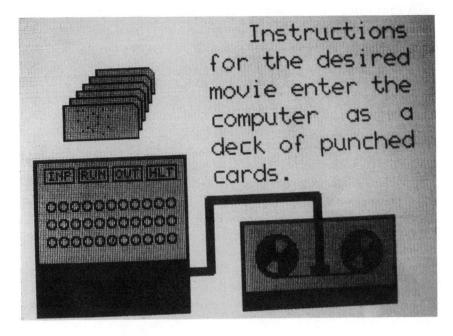

Instructions for the desired movie enter the computer as a deck of punched cards.

1964 animation still. Dr. Kenneth Knowlton.

Collaborations between scientists and artists were recognized as creative requisites and thus encouraged at Bell Laboratories. Liaisons such as that of Stan VanderBeek and Ken Knowlton, as well as Ken Knowlton and Lillian Schwartz, were the embodiment of this influence.

Knowlton and VanderBeek's first collaboration was "Poem Field One" in 1964, the first in a series entitled "Poem Field One through Poem Field Ten"; it was the first of 11 computer films produced by this duo. Eugene Youngblood describes a Poem Field:

The term "Poem Field" indicates the visual effect of the mosaic picture system called BEFLIX (derived from "Bell Flicks") written by Knowlton.

The VanderBeek-Knowlton "Poem Fields" are complex, syncretistic two-dimensional tapestries of geometrical configurations in mosaic patterns. The early "Poem Fields" were investigations of calligraphic relationships between dogs and alphabetic characters integrated into fields of geometrical patterns constantly evolving into new forms. (Youngblood 1970, 266 & 249)

The "Poem Field" series was filmed in black and white and was colored later using an optical printing process.

Knowlton's collaboration with another artist, Lillian Schwartz, was the result of an invitation by co-worker Leon Harmon for Schwartz to visit Bell Laboratories. Schwartz had seen a computer graphic mural by Knowlton and Harmon which was exhibited at the Museum of Modern Art's "Machine" exhibition in 1968 and consequently met Harmon, which led to an introduction to Knowlton (Knowlton, telephone interview, 4 March 1989).

The Knowlton-Schwartz collaboration created a total of ten films from 1970 to 1974. The first two films were produced in 1970, *UFO's,* and *Pixillation. Olympiad,* was the only film made in 1971, but five followed in 1972: *Affinities, Enigma, Googolplex, Apotheosis,* and *Mutations.* In 1973 they produced three computer animations: *Papillons, Innocence,* and *Metamorphosis.* All were created at Bell Laboratories in Murray Hill, New Jersey.

Scientist and artist A. Michael Noll entered the computer animation arena in 1965, producing three films: *4-Dimensional Hypercube, 4-D Hypermovie,* and *Computer-Generated Ballet.* As Cynthia Goodman stated in her book *Digital Visions:*

> He [Noll] pioneered three-dimensional movies (seen in stereoscopic views) and wrote programs for computer-generated choreography and holography. (1987, 26)

Noll's research on four-dimensional hypercubes laid the groundwork for current mathematicians such as Thomas Banchoff to pursue the visualization of four-dimensional geometric forms.

Noll's firm beliefs concerning the history of this medium emerged during an interview:

> I'm a strong believer of giving credit, particularly to pioneers who stick their necks out and frequently don't get any rewards for it. . . . The places early work was going on were Bell Labs and Lawrence Livermore—the people at Bell Labs were Frank Sinden, Ed Zajac, and Ken Knowlton. Those were very important people in terms of animation . . . Sinden's name you never read much about. (personal interview, 9 May 1988)

Other scientists at Bell Laboratories who were involved in different aspects of computer animation were Frank Sinden, Bella Julesz, and C. Bosche. Julesz and Bosche produced computer animations in 1966

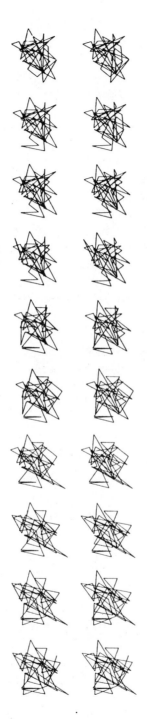

Sequence from a three-dimensional movie of a random line pattern. A. Michael Noll.

and 1967 to aid their experiments in human vision and stereo perception research. Sinden, a physicist, produced *Force, Mass and Motion,* one of the earliest films illustrating physical phenomenon. Made in 1966, the film illustrated Newton's laws of motion.

Lawrence Livermore National Laboratories

Lawrence Livermore's entrance into computer animation came in the late 1950s. In an interview with George Michael, he described the equipment and the sequence of events which led to his research group's use of computer animation:

> Our first display device was attached to an IBM 704 in 1956. There were three of us who were working on it, but it was difficult to get time on the machine. There was no question that being able to see pictures was valuable! Right away we tried to make color movies. A way to do that for us was to collect all the information that was ultimately going to be projected in each color and segregate it one color per frame. I then took the film down to a regular animation place down in Hollywood. They thought we were crazy, but it came out all right. The first colors weren't very good, but we got better. (personal interview, 5 August 1988)

Livermore's earliest use of computer animation was related to weapons research, which is one reason why their work is often omitted from discussions of the pioneer computer animation period. Not only were outsiders unaware of their computer animation work, but people within the lab were also in the dark. As Michael acknowledged, "We stole time! It was considered a piracy action." However, one colleague who was aware of George Michael's work at Livermore was A. Michael Noll. He recollected:

> Another promising place was certainly Lawrence Livermore Laboratory, and in it, George Michael. They were doing computer animation to plot the results of simulations of what looked to me like explosions.

> Computer animation became an absolutely beautiful way to show the results of equations. They would do simulations so that you could see the shock waves and get a physical, graphical sense, which they could never get from equations. (personal interview, 9 May 1988)

George Michael described the work done at Livermore more generally.

. . . in the generic sense, it was used in the solution of differential equations. We were solving fluid flow problems, heat flow problems and some
particle dynamics problems. (personal interview, 5 August 1988)

Another pioneer in scientific computer animation who joined Lawrence Livermore Laboratory in 1977 is mathematician Nelson Max.
His films range from molecule animations to computer animations
which illustrate mathematical functions such as *Carla's Island*.

Although Michael and Max both employ computer animation and
work at Lawrence Livermore Laboratory, they do not share the same
facilities, nor do they collaborate.

Jet Propulsion Laboratory

The Jet Propulsion Laboratory (JPL) graphics laboratory was established in 1975 by Robert Holzman. Holzman, who arrived at JPL
in 1962, reviews the events that led up to the installation of the
graphics laboratory:

At the time I was managing all of the non-space-related activities of the
data systems division. And it seemed that everything that was coming up
needed graphics. We didn't have graphics capability, so I kept complain-
ing. They came to me when they found all this extra money and asked
me to buy some graphics equipment. (personal interview, 27 June 1988)

This "extra money" was the result of new accounting procedures
which JPL was adopting. This resulted in the opportunity for Holzman not only to purchase equipment, such as Evans and Sutherland's
Picture System 2 and frame buffer, but to hire employees. His first
employee was James Blinn. Holzman recalls:

About the same time Ivan Sutherland came to CalTech to take over the
beginning of the computer science department, I talked to him at the
beginning of 1977. He recommended a young graduate student that was
getting his Ph.D. at University of Utah, who was looking for a job on
the west coast. That was Jim Blinn. I talked to Jim, I liked him, and I
hired him. He was my first employee of the graphics lab. (personal
interview, 27 June 1988)

JPL's graphics lab has been the center of much computer animation
creativity both for scientific and artistic purposes. Along with the

images created by James Blinn, the planetary flybys for the Voyager I simulations, his illustrations for the *Mechanical Universe* series, and the sequence for Carl Sagan's television series, which won Blinn an Emmy (Jankel and Morton 14), one must also consider the work of artist in residence, David Em. In 1987, a book of Em's computer "paintings," *The Art of David Em,* debuted.

Both Blinn and Em utilize the programs designed by Blinn, but with very different objectives. Although Blinn has an artistic sense, his goal is to communicate or to inform. He refers to this in an 1987 interview.

> At this point I'm more interested in getting ideas across, rather than just making pictures. I'm more directed by the message I want to get across than by what you can do with the tool. (personal interview, 15 December 1987)

Em uses the same tools to create futuristic landscape paintings. Through the use of the computer, he is able to generate creative visual work.

Ohio State University

The Ohio State University's Computer Graphics Research Group was established by Charles Csuri in 1971. It was the outgrowth of Csuri's art background and interest in computer graphics. The effect of this combination was a unique computer graphics program, which from its inception has had a strong emphasis on the cooperative relationship between art and technology in the creation of images and the development of software programs. Csuri explains:

> Because of my art background, [which] was the primary influence, I started out using the computer as an expressive medium, as an artist. It was later that I began to understand other implications of the computer, in terms of what graphics would do for scientific computing, and for a lot of different applications. Then I started to understand the science in back of it. (personal interview, 18 November 1987)

The program evolved from a few students taking an independent study course from Csuri, into an MFA program in computer graphics. Csuri recalls:

I encouraged some art students to take an independent study with me. I got a handful of students to do that. I gave them access to the computer. Eventually one of them graduated. 1969/1970, that's when we actually got the graduate program going. (personal interview, 18 November 1987)

This evolution later led to the formation of one of the pioneer computer animation production houses, Cranston-Csuri. In addition to being one of the first commercial computer animation production houses, Cranston-Csuri was also attempting to inaugurate a model cooperative relationship between academe and industry. It was proposing a working relationship between a university (Ohio State University) and a production company (Cranston-Csuri Productions). Csuri, in an interview, describes the attempt as

trying to establish a relationship between the university and the company. We were put into this building, the approval was given by the president of the university. He wanted to see whether or not we could make it work; a productive relationship between industry and the University. I was the trial balloon, I was an experiment, in terms of my operation. (personal interview, 18 November 1987)

Csuri's first computer animation was *Hummingbird,* which was produced in 1967 with digitized hand-drawn images of a hummingbird (personal interview, 18 November 1987). The computer's role was in the manipulation or movement of the drawings, not in the generation of images. In 1970 Csuri developed a real-time computer animation system (Csuri 1970, 289-305), which was replaced two years later, in 1972, by Tom DeFanti's Graphics Symbiosis System, known more widely as GRASS. DeFanti, who founded the University of Illinois' Electronic Visualization Laboratory, was at the time a doctoral student of Csuri's.

Ohio State University's Computer Graphics Research Group has been the center for many developments in computer animation such as Anima, a 3-D real-time animation system developed by Charles Csuri in 1975, and the Skeleton Animation System, SAS, which focuses on human motion. SAS was developed in 1982 by David Zeltzer.

Cranston-Csuri was responsible for some of the most realistic computer animation illustrating the human body and its movement, exhibited extensively in the television series *The Body Machine.* In it, "images of the human torso, eyeball, heart, colon, and male sexual organs" (Jankel and Morton 1984, 76) were depicted. The series was produced in 1983 by Goldcrest Films (Jankel and Morton 1984, 67).

University of Utah

The University of Utah dominated computer graphics research during the 1960s and early 1970s as a center of hardware and software development. This is apparent not only from the equipment and programs which were designed, but by the individuals who were products of that institution, such as Ed Catmull, Fred Parke, James Blinn, and Frank Crow. One major reason for the level of productivity was the unspoken expectation of mentors David Evans and Ivan Sutherland. Ed Catmull explains:

> In this program the expectation was to advance the state of the art of computer graphics when you did your dissertation. (personal interview, 19 May 1988)

Ed Catmull's contributions included the Z buffer and an algorithm for computer display of curved surfaces (Catmull 1974). James Blinn improved curved surface techniques and texture mapping (Ed Catmull, personal interview, 19 May 1988), and Fred Parke contributed to the animation of human faces, including speech synchronization (Parke 1972).

After leaving MIT and serving in the Department of Defense, Ivan Sutherland arrived at the University of Utah in the early 1960s with his continued interest in interactive computer systems intact. Utah appeared to be an appropriate place to continue his interest in computer animation. As Judson Rosebush stated in his history:

> The Utah facility was able to generate film animation, again using filters and a custom CRT. Several animated films were made using this facility; some of the more unusual done by Fred Parke involved animations of talking faces and figures. (1979, 24)

During this period, David Evans and Ivan Sutherland founded Evans and Sutherland Computer Corporation, which manufactured graphic display systems and began building frame buffers in 1973 (Rosebush 1979, 30). Because of the relationship between the company's founders and the University of Utah, there is a cooperative alliance between these organizations which has affected the development of computer graphics and computer animation technology.

The industry-academe association which Charles Csuri and Ohio State University attempted to found appears instead to have been achieved by the University of Utah and Evans and Sutherland. The result is a strong cooperative force which has encouraged research in specific areas and established the University of Utah and Evan and Sutherland as leaders in hidden surface, curve surfaces, and texture mapping, and earlier as the manufacturers of the first commercial frame buffer.

Currently Evans and Sutherland products offer applications in mechanical CAD/CAM, molecular modeling, aircraft and auto design, medical imaging, plant design, seismic and petroleum research, and avionics laboratory systems.

4

Pioneer Period

The pioneer period of computer animation embodied two major elements, technical discoveries and the emergence of individual pioneers. From these two categories emanated a wealth of applications which include military applications, simulations, conceptual illustrations, and artistic explorations.

Computer graphics and computer animation's foundation lie deeply rooted in military science. One of the earliest uses of computer graphics was in air defense. SAGE, Semi Automatic Ground Environment (Fichera 1988, II-2), a United States government air defense system, was introduced in the 1950s. Jankel and Morton describe it as

> the first example of a production system that relied on the use of interactive computer graphics. Missiles and aircraft were detected by radar and their positions displayed on screens. Operators at these screens examined the images and decided which targets were interesting; these were indicated to the computer by pointing at them with a light pen. The computer then performed tracking and interception calculations, and relayed the results to command stations elsewhere. (1984, 18-19)

There were two reasons for this tie with the military: The first was timing, for most of these developments took place during World War II or immediately following and were related to radar detection; at that time there was still great concern over national security. The second reason was economics. These systems were very expensive; private resources could not afford them, however, the government, via tax dollars, could.

The second application computer animation was widely used for was simulation, primarily simulation of aircraft landings, takeoffs, and emergency procedures. Practices and testing were indeed much more cost-effective. As computer graphics historian Patric Prince stated in a discussion on the pioneer period of computer graphics:

A lot of the early research and development was based on landing aircraft because it was cheaper to simulate takeoffs and landings than crashing. (personal interview, 12 January 1988)

Computer animation's ability to illustrate concepts and visualize mathematical abstractions was discovered early on. Frank Sinden's computer animation on Newton's theories and A. Michael Noll's four-dimensional animations are examples of these applications.

The discovery of this medium's potential as a new art-making tool was grasped immediately. Artists, as well as technicians and scientists, began to explore the qualities and characteristics offered by this new communication resource. The collaborative works of Stan Vander-Beek and Ken Knowlton, and Lillian Schwartz and Ken Knowlton are examples of such investigations, along with the solo explorations of John Whitney, Sr.

Technical Discoveries

There were three major technical innovations that took place during the pioneer period which heralded the ability to create computer animations. They included

the electronic microfilm recorder that, with the computer that controls it, draws 100,000 points, lines, or characters or several frames of simple line drawings per second.

A second technical innovation was an automation computer program developed by Ron Baecker of Lincoln Labs, that allows the artist to erase, add details, cull, and move in on detail.

A third innovation was a special computer language called BEFLIX, developed by Ken Knowlton of Bell Laboratories. (Russett and Starr 1976, 199)

These advances laid the groundwork for the development of computer animation. The microfilm recorder offered the opportunity to document and preserve images generated on the computer. It also presented the ability to create animation. As A. Michael Noll explains:

The microfilm plotter photographs the images on the CRT and produces a strip of 35mm film. If you do those photographs as a series, slightly changing from each other and then run them through a 35mm projector, or convert to 16mm, you have a movie, which is what I did. (personal interview, 9 May 1988)

The other advantage offered was the flexibility to experiment; as Ken Knowlton comments:

Because of their high speeds of calculation and display, the computer and automatic film recorder make feasible the production of some kinds of films that previously would have been far too expensive or difficult. In addition, the speed, ease, and economy of computer animation permit the moviemaker to take several tries at a scene—producing a whole family of film clips—from which he chooses the most appealing result, a luxury never before possible. (1968, 67-68)

The computer animation program developed by Ron Baecker provided capabilities similar to direct-method animation offerings to pioneer experimental filmmakers, where one draws directly on the film. The difference is that in this case the user draws directly on the screen to create images.

Ken Knowlton's BEFLIX (Knowlton's variation on "Bell Flicks"), was an animation language designed for making computer films. BEFLIX was Stan VanderBeek's introduction to computer animation. Knowlton and VanderBeek's collaborative films, the *Poem Field* series and the film they produced for Expo '67, *Man and His World,* were all produced with BEFLIX. In an interview, VanderBeek commented on the artists response to this new tool:

For the artist, moving into the area of computers is extending his mind with a tool technically as responsive as himself.

An abstract motion system for making movies and image storage and retrieval systems open a door to a kind of mental attitude of moviemaking—the artist is no longer restricted to the exact execution of form. (Russett and Starr 1976, 201)

One final technical innovation which guided the development of computer animation is the frame buffer. The name, as explained by Fox and Waite,

comes from the fact that the device is a large memory designed to hold a single frame of film, a graphic picture. (1984, 57)

The frame buffer is a device which allows the user to view previous images on the monitor. One of the first frame buffers, which was three bits, was built at Bell Laboratories in 1969. However, Richard Shoup, who was at Xerox PARC in Palo Alto, built the first eight-bit frame buffer in 1972. Alvy Ray Smith recalls:

> The only frame buffer that existed was Dick Shoup's. He built the first serious one. There were some three–bit ones, but he had the first eight–bit frame buffer with graphical abilities, with tablet input, and video output. It was a whole system, color maps and the whole thing. (personal interview, 19 May 1988)

Judson Rosebush confirms this assertion:

> The Xerox machine [frame buffer] had look-up tables for indexing colors and may be considered the first 'modern' machine. (1979, 29)

Evans and Sutherland Computer Corporation was the first company to manufacture frame buffers. They began manufacturing the first commercial frame buffers in 1973. The first models were sold to the New York Institute of Technology in 1974 (Alvy Ray Smith, personal interview, 19 May 1988).

Individual Pioneers

There are several prominent pioneers in computer animation: John Whitney, Sr., Kenneth Knowlton, A. Michael Noll, Ivan Sutherland, Charles Csuri, Lillian Schwartz, and the late Stan VanderBeek. Each contributed not only his or her individual work, but a step towards the development of the medium as well. This group of individuals, like most assemblages of talent in computer animation, is a combination of scientists and artists who defy categories—for many practice in both disciplines and have answered to both titles at one time or another.

Five of these seven pioneers were interviewed for this study. Ivan Sutherland declined to be interviewed, and Stan VanderBeek died previous to this inquiry. Therefore, individual profiles on John Whitney, Sr., Kenneth Knowlton, A. Michael Noll, and Charles Csuri follow. A profile on Lillian Schwartz will appear later, in the artists section.

JOHN WHITNEY, SR.

One of the earliest pioneers in computer animation was experimental animator John Whitney, Sr. He and his brother James began making experimental films in the 1940s in addition to designing and building their own equipment. In the late 1940s they created a series of films entitled *The Five Abstract Film Exercises,* which was exhibited worldwide and won first prize at the First Experimental Film Competition in Belgium.

In the early 1950s, Whitney, Sr. began making a series of engineering films on guided missiles for what was then Douglas Aircraft. In 1957 he collaborated with Charles Eames in establishing a seven-screen presentation for the Buckminster Fuller Dome in Moscow (Russett and Starr 1976, 180).

His work with Saul Bass, which included animating the title sequence for Alfred Hitchcock's film *Vertigo* served as his introduction to Hollywood. In 1960 he founded Motion Graphics Inc., a company which produced film and television title sequences and commercials. The predominant tool used for these projects was the mechanical analog computer he and his brother James designed and built from World War II anti-aircraft surplus supplies. He recalled:

> By 1957 or 1958 I was on to these analog computing devices that were used as anti-aircraft gun directors, and aware of the fact that I was able, for pennies, to buy mechanical equipment that's unbelievably costly . . . somehow, the possibilities for a very flexible design tool, which should be the thing of my interest, instead of trying to improve cameras or develop other camera techniques. And that led me into developing my animation machine. (Russett and Starr 1976, 184)

John Whitney, Sr. has been the recipient of many fellowships and awards throughout the years including a 1962 fellowship from the Graham Foundation for Advanced Study in the Fine Arts, a Guggenheim Fellowship, and a residency at the Center for Advanced Visual Studies at MIT. He also received a three-year research grant from IBM to study motion design using IBM's digital equipment.

One of the products of Whitney Sr.'s IBM research grant was his film *Permutations*. In a description of *Permutations* Whitney, Sr. declared:

> The film contains various types of dot patterns which might be compared
> to the alphabet. The patterns are constructed into 'words' . . . These words
> in turn can be fitted contextually into 'sentence' structures. My use of the
> parallel to language is only partially descriptive; I am moved to draw
> parallels with music. (Youngblood 1970, 215)

Whitney's book *Digital Harmony,* which was published in 1980,
describes the basis of his work. He states in the foreword:

> The foundation of my work rests first upon laws of harmony, then in
> turn, upon proof that the harmony is matched, part for part, in a world
> of visual design. (Whitney 1980, 5)

In an 1987 interview, during a discussion concerning his thesis, Whitney, Sr. asserted that a universality of this harmonic hypothesis exists.
He also posits that presently there are many misconceptions regarding
its origins:

> In this century a lot of understanding actually was lost. [In] Twentieth
> century modern music, there was an effort made to say that harmonic
> relationships were not important. But harmony is the foundation and it
> is universal. A lot of college textbooks on music say that it's western
> culture that has used harmonic relationships, but that's not true at all. It
> is not peculiar to western, it's African, it's Chinese. It was realized in the
> sixth century B.C. Pythagoras was already so sophisticated as to state that
> those intervals can be explained in terms of numbers. (John Whitney, Sr.,
> personal interview, 17 December 1987)

Although Whitney is responsible for the design and construction
of early analog computer animation tools, and has worked in film and
video, he claims to have no preference in media, but instead, prefers
to focus on his interest:

> My interests have been from the very beginning nothing to do with these
> technical matters. I've been interested in making musical experience that
> would be visible. I've been interested in the idea of visual music, whatever
> the medium. (John Whitney, Sr., personal interview, 17 December 1987)

A review of Whitney's work elucidates both his ability and his need
to collaborate. His first collaboration was with his brother James in

the early years while developing equipment and producing experimental films. Later in the mid-sixties Whitney began to work with IBM physicist Dr. Jack Citron. This collaboration led to his residency at IBM and Citron's creation of "GRAF," the Fortran program which was written specifically for Whitney. "GRAF" is an acronym for Graphic Additions to Fortran (Youngblood 1970, 216). In the early 1970s Whitney had access to Information International Inc.'s equipment (more commonly known as Triple I). This arrangement, which also included a programmer, was probably the result of his son John Whitney, Jr's position with the company. His film *Matrix 3* was the product of that arrangement. However, the subsequent arrangement with Triple I did not include the use of a programmer, and Whitney's next collaborator was computer animator Larry Cuba, who provided the programming for "Arabesque." Cuba recalls:

He [Whitney] called me up and said he had gotten computer time at Triple I again. The last film he [Whitney] had made at that time was *Matrix 3,* which was done at Triple I and they supplied him with the equipment and a programmer. This time around, they were going to let him use the equipment, but they couldn't spare the body. So he asked me if I would program for him. And we made this arrangement that I would program his film and in return I would get access to Triple I's equipment. (personal interview, 18 January 1988)

Yet another collaborator, Paul Rother, was responsible for Whitney's Pascal programming in the late 1970s (Whitney 1980, 9).

Pioneer, innovator, and creator of computer animation, Whitney's accomplishments include an additional contribution: He is also the father of three sons who have been involved with film animation and technology from childhood on. His eldest son, John Whitney, Jr., has also been a key figure in the development and use of computer animation; his role and contributions will be discussed later.

KENNETH KNOWLTON

In 1962, immediately after completing his Ph.D. at MIT in communication sciences, Kenneth Charles Knowlton began his twenty-year career at Bell Laboratories. In describing this introductory period he states:

There was this microfilm printer there, so very quickly I started making pictures and getting into programming languages. (telephone interview, 4 March 1989)

Knowlton developed the first computer animation language in 1965. "BEFLIX," named for Bell Flicks, was a computer technique for producing animated movies. Thalmann and Thalmann describe "BEFLIX's" unconventional, nonmathematical approach to the generation of computer animation:

> There are almost no mathematics in BEFLIX. Animation is completed by sending electronic signals (waves) to make image distortions. . . . As BEFLIX contains little mathematics, Ken Knowlton has combined this language with Fortran IV. This produced the Fortran IV BEFLIX animated movie language which is quite powerful for its time. (1985, 19–20)

BEFLIX was used in the production of many films, including the collaborative *Poem Fields* series by Stan VanderBeek and Ken Knowlton.

Knowlton's collaborations began with Bell Laboratory's visual perception researcher, Leon Harmon; the product was a series of studies in perception. This series included such images as a "gargoyle, a telephone, and two flying seagulls" (Goodman 1987, 34) as well as the most famous image, a twelve-foot nude of dancer Deborah Hay, which was exhibited at the New York Museum of Modern Art. The exhibition, "The Machine as Seen at the End of the Mechanical Age," was curated by K. G. Pontus Hulten. The images generated by Knowlton and Harmon were based on photographs which were digitized and then manipulated with Knowlton's picture-processing method.

Other collaborators include artist Stan VanderBeek, whose joint efforts with Knowlton produced over twelve films, including a film for Expo '67, *Man and His World*. Knowlton's final collaborator was artist Lillian Schwartz, whom he worked with from 1971 through 1975. Their eleven joint ventures won numerous film awards.

These collaborative efforts illustrate Knowlton's advocacy of the cooperative needs of computer animation. In a 1970 article in Filmmakers Newsletter he argued that

> we need to develop a great deal of collaboration between artists and programmers in order to develop meaningful, understandable, and useful sets of tools and ways of using them. (Russett and Starr 1976, 195)

Knowlton's present position is a bit different, for he appears to be putting more responsibility on the artists, as revealed in a 1989 interview:

A lot [*sic*] better interface between artists and machine is needed so artists can become more expressive and learn how to use these tools. (telephone interview, 4 March 1989)

Knowlton left Bell Laboratories in 1982 and is presently working at Wang Laboratories in Lowell, Massachusetts. He is currently working on a project which he describes as "a product that has to do with office technology, the paperless office" (telephone interview, 4 March 1989).

As previously stated in the beginning of this section, the divisions between artist and scientist fade very quickly in this medium. (This was especially true for the pioneers.) Yet, while much has been written about the pioneering technical developments of Ken Knowlton, the artistic side of the man is usually excluded. Pioneer software developer and former Bell Laboratories researcher Turner Whitted revealed another side of Ken Knowlton:

> Ken Knowlton has always been one of my heroes. He's one of the smartest people I've ever met. But the fact that he considers himself an artist was a shock to me. I thought of Ken as an engineer, a physicist, as a scientist that did animation on the side. His collaborations with Lillian Schwartz were technical and artistic collaborations. After I got to know him better, I realized that Ken really is an artist. In fact, he thinks of himself more as an artist than he does as a scientist. To him, computer science is how you pay the bills, being an artist is what he really is. (Turner Whitted, personal interview, 1 August 1988)

A. MICHAEL NOLL

A. Michael Noll's attraction to computer imaging was the product of a childhood interest in drawing and graphics, but with a different focus. He explains:

> As a child I was always interested in drawing and graphics, in particular more mechanical drawing, where things were more ordered and structured types of things as opposed to free-flowing things. (personal interview, 9 May 1988)

Noll received a B.S. in Electrical Engineering from the Newark College of Engineering in 1961, which led to a research position at Bell Laboratories in Murray Hill, New Jersey. His research focus was man-machine communications, speech processing, and computer graphics. In 1963 he received an M.E.E. from New York University, and in 1971 he was awarded a Ph.D. in Electrical Engineering from the Polytechnic Institute of Brooklyn. His thesis title was *Man-Machine Tactile Communication*.

Noll's introduction to computer graphics was the result of Bell Laboratories' acquisition of a microfilm plotter. He recalls:

> Bell Labs had a microfilm plotter, which they had just recently acquired. They were using it for text. They had a way of putting it on the face of the CRT and photographing that, but also it could do scientific plots, curves, and drawings, and it became natural to use it for graphics. (personal interview, 9 May 1988)

A childhood toy, the 3-D viewer, introduced Noll to stereoscopic and three-dimensional perspectives, which later lead him to pursue research on three-dimensional and stereoscopic imaging. Noll explains:

> I was always interested in 3-D, and 3-D viewers; I grew up looking at them. The idea of using the computer to calculate separate images for the left eye and the right eye occurred to me and so I started doing that. I had all sorts of 3-D slides, all sorts of random objects; sculptures I called them. (personal interview, 9 May 1988)

Three-dimensional images are created by

> presenting two slightly different pictures separately to each eye. These two pictures are the perspective projections of some object as seen from two slightly different positions. Although the two perspectives are quite similar, the human brain translates their minute differences into a very realistic depth effect. (A. M. Noll 1965, 20)

This intrigue with 3-D objects and images led quite naturally into the generation of three-dimensional films. Noll expounds:

> Other people at the Bell Labs started doing movies. It was the obvious thing to do. The microfilm plotter produces a strip of 35mm film, which photographs the images on the CRT . . . I started doing 3-D movies. Rather than making just a single image, two images were combined in a frame. Then you could look at those with special glasses and a special adapter for the projector. All this was in the early 1960's, 1963 or 1964. (personal interview, 9 May 1988)

In 1965 Noll, Frieder Nake, and George Nees arranged for the first computer-generated art exhibition. It was held in Stuttgart, Germany at the Technische Hochschule (Goodman 1987, 23). In that same year, Noll participated in a two-man "Computer-Generated Pictures" art exhibit with Bela Julesz, also from Bell Laboratories, at the Howard Wise Gallery in New York City.

Noll was one of the first scientists or mathematicians to contemplate the use of the computer to visualize mathematical concepts in multidimensional space. His four-dimensional computer animation research laid the groundwork for later mathematicians such as Thomas Banchoff and Heinz Otto-Peitgen who employ computer animation as their primary research tool.

Although Noll did not pursue his early four-dimensional hypercube research, current researchers value his foundation work. Thomas Banchoff revealed:

> I should say that we used some of the earlier work Michael Noll had done, a film on the four-dimensional hypercube. He wrote a paper about it, in which he very obligingly gave his evaluation of what he had done. He said although they thought it was going to help to understand, it didn't. I guess we felt he wasn't looking at the right things, because it does help, it did help and continues to help. It's helped a generation of mathematicians. It certainly helped me understand things that I couldn't understand before. (personal interview, 3 August 1988)

Noll furthered his study of stereoscopic images and computer animation by combining them and then investigating another element, interactivity. He explains:

> I got interested in interactive three-dimensional displays. We did that in real time. I was working with a three-dimensional joystick, a 3-D controller. You could reach into a three-dimensional space and latch on to things. It was like a three-dimensional sketchpad. So you could do true stereoscopic drawing. And that led me to the idea of using motors to control the input device, so that in addition to moving around in three-dimensional space, you could feel where you were. The computer would issue signals to control the motors and you would feel as though you had bumped into things. That was probably done about 1969 to 1971. (personal interview, 9 May 1988)

Noll left Bell Laboratories in 1971 and worked as a technical assistant in the White House Office of Science and Technology. He returned to Bell Laboratories in 1973, but abandoned his research in computer graphics.

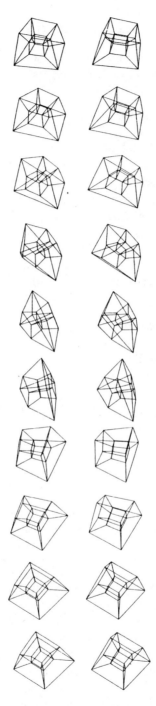

Selected frame from a movie of the three-dimensional projection of a rotating four-dimensional hypercube. A. Michael Noll.

I was interested more in the problem of peoples' use of technology. I was much more interested in marketing and I was realizing that technology is not the answer to all of the world's problems. So I became interested in trying to match peoples' needs with technology. (A. Michael Noll, personal interview, 9 May 1988)

Ingrained in Michael Noll is the need to pursue new problems, discover new ground. As he reveals: "I personally get bored with doing the same things" (personal interview, 9 May 1988). Presently, at the University of Southern California in the Annenberg School for Communication, Noll currently addresses the problem of technological illiteracy in his work. He explains:

Now I'm doing something new again. I'm in education and the problem I'm worrying about is illiteracy towards technology. So through books and courses, I'm doing my best to try and solve that problem and show people that non-technical people can learn and understand the basics and principles of technology. (personal interview, 9 May 1988)

CHARLES A. CSURI

Charles Csuri was trained as a traditional artist in painting at the Ohio State University in Columbus, Ohio, earning an A.B. in Art and Industrial Design in 1947 and an M.F.A. in Art in 1948. He was a classmate and friend of both pop artist Roy Lichtenstein and sculptor George Segal. His introduction to computers came in the early 1950s. He recalled:

In approximately 1955 I became aware of computers. That was through a personal friend in the university, a professor of engineering. We had a continuing discussion for ten years, about computers, and what impact it would have on society, and what it might conceivably mean for the arts. Once I became aware of the graphic output device, then it was as if ten years of thinking came together. (personal interview, 18 November 1987)

Csuri's last body of artwork before embarking into computer graphics was a preamble to the computer: He designed an analog device on which he produced a series of variations or transformations, as he refers to them, on a drawing. Describing this work he states:

Before I went to the computer, the last artwork I was doing, I had designed a machine, an analog device to make transformations on a drawing. It was based upon the principle of the pentagram. I did a whole series of drawings like that just before I went into the computer. So I was working with analog techniques and some mathematical ideas even in my more traditional medium. (personal interview, 18 November 1987)

Csuri's art background has been the driving force not only in his own computer graphic work, but in the Computer Research Group and the Advanced Computing Center for Arts and Design, both of which he established at Ohio State University. Csuri reveals:

> Because of my art background, that was my primary influence, I started out using the computer as an expressive medium, as an artist. It was later that I began to understand other implications of the computer, in terms of what graphics would do for scientific computing and for a lot of different applications. Then I began to understand the science in back of it, and got interested in it and pursued grants. (personal interview, 18 November 1987)

It was this later cognizance that prompted the foundation of Ohio State University's Computer Research Group, and the realization that in order to accomplish "anything in the arts," (Charles Csuri, personal interview, 18 November 1987) research support would have to be obtained. Although Csuri studied mathematics and physics while in the army engineering accelerated program, he did not possess the technical expertise necessary for computers. Therefore, Csuri had to seek the abilities of others, and responded by building a corps of technicians and artists. He explains:

> I didn't have the technical background that I really needed, and so I had to think in terms of building a team of people to work with me. That meant getting money, getting resources, and so that's the path I've taken. (personal interview, 18 November 1987)

Members of Csuri's "team" included at one time: Tom DeFanti, co-director of the Electronic Visualization Laboratory at the University of Illinois and developer of the GRASS animation system; David Zeltzer, developer of SAS (the skeleton animation system); Michael Collery, who is presently with Pacific Data Images; and researcher Frank Crow, who is currently part of a research team at Xerox PARC.

Csuri's background, and his insight into the fundamental properties essential to computer animation, in conjunction with his early interest in the medium, provided the necessary resources and talent to establish one of the most creative cooperative environments for computer animation.

5

Introductory Period

Computer animation's introductory period encompasses the sequence of events representing this medium's debut into the mass media. It covers computer animation's launch into advertising, as well as its entry into the commercial film entertainment industry.

Secondly, and equally significant, this era also marked the commencement of a great pursuit for realism. Judson Rosebush explains:

> The end of the 1960s saw an impressive range of problems recognized and addressed. The decade began with the simplest vector animation and culminated with full-color systems. The next decade would witness a striving for more explicit realism, an embellishment of techniques, and new methods. (1979, 25-26)

Third, and finally, it offered a simulated realistic view of the universe. Through the talents of James Blinn, the world had the opportunity to visit Jupiter, Saturn, Uranus, and Neptune, by visually tracking the U.S. space missions. Animation historian, Charles Solomon asserts that:

> Blinn's simulated fly-bys for NASA have given TV audiences a clearer vision of the solar system and a better understanding of our efforts to explore it. (1983, 6)

And, through the gifted efforts of Nelson Max, one could observe previously unseen vantage points of geometric forms.

The first commercial use of computer animation is attributed to Mathematical Applications Group Inc. (MAGI), for an IBM advertisement (Randy Randall, personal interview, 12 January 1988). Phillip Mittelman, founder of MAGI, recalls:

> The first job we ever did was in early 1969—maybe 1970, for IBM. They had an office products division and they wanted to have a film showing

Still from *Planet*. Dr. James F. Blinn.

letters flying around, as though they were coming out of the word processor. It was black and white. (personal interview, 11 May 1988)

MAGI, joined later by Robert Abel and Associates, Information International Inc. (Triple I), and Digital Effects, became the modern-day town criers. These forerunners employed a new form of mass communication which seemed to project the high-tech, slick, modern twentieth-century image which many of the Fortune 500 companies were attempting to emulate.

The feature film *Westworld*, produced in 1973, was computer animation's serious entrée into entertainment film (Wilson 1986, 21). Computer generated images representing the robot's point of view were the creation of John Whitney Jr., Gary Demos, and Richard Taylor, all part of Triple I's Entertainment Technology Group. These individuals were responsible for pushing this new visual special effects trend in feature films (Jankel and Morton 1984, 111). Their second attempt, the 1976 sequel, *Futureworld*, displayed a computer generated bust of actor Peter Fonda. This technique was further developed and used in a 1981 film, *LOOKER,* to produce a full-body simulation of actress Susan Dey.

During this introduction period, computer animation was used to sell ideas and products, to illustrate new perceptions of the world, to aid in the visualization of other planets, and to create new realities. As a result of its debut in film and television, for the first time computer animation had the ability to influence not only a select few, but the masses.

Technical Advances

The technical advances of this introductory period center on one issue, the pursuit of increased objective reality. This goal encompassed the search for efficient algorithms to remove hidden surfaces and aliasing (the jagged staircase effect), as well as algorithms to aid in improved texture and shading of two- and three-dimensional images. Judson Rosebush asserts:

> The strive[ing] for more realistic computer images has forced a reappraisal of fundamental techniques, such as hidden surface removal. (1979, 28)

> Underlying this period was a search for a fast algorithm to remove hidden surfaces—an admitted computational bottleneck. (1979, 20)

Three individuals led the research in hidden and curved surfaces, texture, shading, and shadows: Ed Catmull, Frank Crow, and James Blinn. All were products of the University of Utah's computer science program.

Frank Crow's 1977 pioneer work defined the aliasing problem in computer generated images (1977, 799-805). He went on to develop anti-aliasing and shading algorithms (1977b, 242-48). Crow stresses that his role in computer animation has been through his algorithm designs, not through the creation of computer animation:

> You could argue that I haven't really been in computer animation. What I've done is produce display algorithms which other people have used to produce animation. (personal interview, 16 May 1988)

Ed Catmull's early research focused on hidden-surface algorithms with anti-aliasing capabilities (1978, 6-11). These findings were recorded in the 1978 SIGGRAPH Proceedings. Recalling his contributions, Catmull states:

I was working on curved surfaces. In doing curved surfaces, I invented the Z buffer, which everybody now uses. I did the display of curved surfaces, which at the time I thought was the most important thing that I did. But in fact, the texture mapping that I developed had a greater effect. (personal interview, 19 May 1988)

James Blinn is responsible for much of the early research on texture mapping and light reflection (1976, 542-47; 1977, 192-98). Ed Catmull credits Blinn with having developed texture mapping and curved surfaces fully: "Jim carried the curved surface and the texture mapping to its maximum" (personal interview, 19 May 1988). These techniques can be seen in Blinn's films, *Voyager 1 Encounters Jupiter,* and *Voyager 2 Encounters Jupiter.*

Another significant technical advance developed during this period at the National Research Council of Canada, was the key frame animation system designed by Nestor Burtnyk and Marceli Wein (Burtnyk and Wein 1971, 149-53). This in-betweening calculation system was the tool which the late artist Peter Foldes utilized to produce his 1974 Cannes award-winning film *Hunger,* as well as two other films *Metadata,* and *Visages.* Marceli Wein describes their initial approach and the equipment used in this project:

The way we came into computing was from engineering. We had a micro computer that we used as a simple user computer. We did not have time sharing. Now, in retrospect, we were using that microcomputer as a workstation, one person at a time. The main communication with the computer was through the screen, so there was very little typing. The graphical interface was there. It was an early workstation.

We made two films in that phase, one was made in 1971 and the other one we worked on and off and finished in 1973. The first film was *Metadata*. That film builds on the early approaches to in-betweening and metamorphosis, changes from images to images—but very little control. (personal interview, 3 August 1988)

Individual Presenters

The presenters are those individuals and computer animation houses who introduced computer animation to the public, who brought it to the public's attention and into their living rooms. The individuals, James Blinn (a scientist) and Nelson Max (a mathematician), used computer animation to present scientific and mathematical information which previously could not be visualized. There were four original, or, as Judson Rosebush designated them, "first generation" computer animation houses: Mathematical Applications Group Inc. (MAGI), Digital Effects, Information International Inc. (Triple I), and Robert Abel and Associates.

> MAGI, Digital Effects, Triple I, and Abel are first generation houses. Cranston-Csuri, Digital Productions, and Omnibus are second generation, and then the third generation houses are the people who came in with the turnkey systems. (Judson Rosebush, personal interview, 5 August 1988)

Jankel and Morton concur with Rosebush's identification of these pioneer computer animation houses:

> The American computer commercial scene stretches from New York to Los Angeles via Indiana and Denver. . . . The facilities which dominate the scene in design and technological terms are the companies which worked on *TRON*—Digital Effects, MAGI, Robert Abel, and Triple I. (1984, 130)

JAMES BLINN

In 1983, James Blinn received the first SIGGRAPH Computer Graphic Achievement Award and a NASA Exceptional Service Medal. These awards are public acknowledgments of his many contributions to computer science and the space effort.

Born and raised in Michigan, James Blinn earned his B.A. and master's degrees from the University of Michigan at Ann Arbor. It was there that Blinn was introduced to computer animation. He recalls:

> I got into computer animation in about 1968 or 1969. I worked on a computer graphics system at University of Michigan and we did real time animation with that, moving things around.

> When I started getting involved with computers in Michigan, there was a project that the National Science Foundation funded called, 'The Conversational Uses of Computers.' It's like interactive computing, and one small subsection of it was experimenting with computer graphics, essentially drawing circuit diagrams and having to analyze them, analyzed

by the computer. I got a job as a programmer on that project. That was around 1967 or 68. (personal interview, 15 December 1987)

Leaving Ann Arbor in 1972 after receiving his master's degree, Blinn entered University of Utah's computer science department, where the study of computer animation and computer graphics was accepted as a respected discipline. He explains:

When I was at Michigan, I tinkered with computer animation and computer graphics, but it was never really considered a valid academic discipline. Whereas at Utah, it was considered a valid academic discipline and it was respectable to do that. (personal interview, 15 December 1987)

While at the University of Utah, Blinn never studied with "the father of computer graphics," pioneer Ivan Sutherland, however, aware of Blinn's work Sutherland once asserted, "There are about a dozen great computer graphics people and Jim Blinn is six of them" (O'Neill 1986, 30).

In 1977 Robert Holzman, who was in the process of establishing the Computer Graphics Laboratory at the Jet Propulsion Laboratory (JPL), consulted Ivan Sutherland, who had just arrived at California Institute of Technology (CalTech) to set up CalTech's computer science department. Sutherland recommended Blinn to Holzman, who was looking for employees for the newly established JPL Graphics Lab. After an initial meeting with Holzman, Blinn became the first employee hired by the graphics laboratory (Robert Holzman, personal interview, 27 June 1988). Thus began Blinn's JPL era.

Blinn, who had been interested in JPL's endeavors for quite some time, had some reservations regarding the usefulness of his work. His concerns were soon alleviated, for after reviewing a film using line drawings to depict the projected view the Voyager spacecraft would observe as it flew by Jupiter, he envisioned his first project. Because of his experience at the University of Utah in texture mapping, he immediately embarked on creating a more realistic flyby simulation of the Voyager spacecraft's passes over Jupiter and Saturn. This was the first of several flyby simulations which Blinn created (James Blinn, personal interview, 15 December 1987).

Blinn's subsequent project was a series of 52 half-hour programs for a television college course, *The Mechanical Universe*. Blinn produced over seven hours and 530 scenes of computer animation for this telecourse which was funded by the Annenberg/CPB Project.

Still from *Mechanical Universe*. Dr. James F. Blinn.

Although he claims no formal training in art, Blinn is the offspring of two artists who are also art teachers. This he offers as partial justification for his intuitive artistic sense which is evident in *Mechanical Universe*. He explains:

> Both my parents are art teachers. They do artwork, but they make their living teaching art. They do painting, pottery, and sculpture. My mother helped design the house we grew up in, my father does sculpture. The house I grew up in is sort of like an art museum. My grandfather also painted and did wood carvings and my other grandfather was a civil engineer. (personal interview, 15 December 1987)

Blinn's last project at the JPL Graphics Laboratory was a mathematical educational series. He described it as

> a project to do educational animation for mathematics. The mathematics series is designed more for classroom use, rather than broadcast. (personal interview, 15 December 1987)

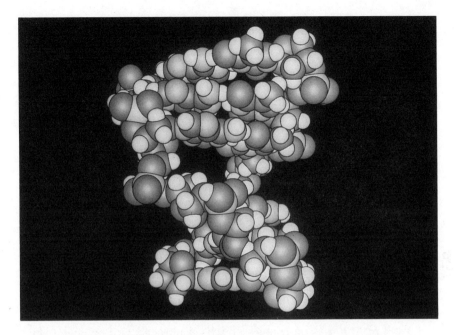

Frame from the film *DNA with Ethidium*. Dr. Nelson L. Max.

Blinn left JPL in October 1988 (R. L. Phillips 1988, 11), and is currently at CalTech completing the high school video mathematics series he began at JPL.

NELSON MAX

In 1963 Nelson Max completed his B.A. at Johns Hopkins University in mathematics. He proceeded to Harvard University, where he received his M.A. in 1964 and his Ph.D. in 1967, both in mathematics, specifically in topology. However, his fascination with mathematics can be traced back to his high school years. He explains:

> I was pretty good in math in high school and so I studied math in college and got a Ph.D. in topology. It's the kind of math dealing with curves and surfaces and higher dimension, and how they fit together. (personal interview, 1 August 1988)

At Harvard, Max's interest in a *Scientific American* article prompted his discovery of computer animation as a useful tool for geometric visualization. He recalls:

While at Harvard, Tony Phillips wrote an article on how to turn a sphere inside out. It was May 1966, in *Scientific American*. (personal interview, 1 August 1988)

In 1969 Max applied for a grant from the National Science Foundation (NSF) to support the production of a computer animated film on how to turn a sphere inside out. The application was returned with suggestions for Max to consult with individuals involved in educational filmmaking. So he began to work with a company which produced physics films—EDC—at which time he also learned how to program for computer graphics. In 1970, Max received an NSF grant and began making films on mathematical concepts, or, as he states it, "I got into computer animation trying to illustrate concepts in topology" (personal interview, 1 August 1988). In 1976 he successfully completed his 23-minute film *Turning a Sphere Inside Out*, the impetus for his entry into computer animation.

Soon after however, Max found himself in a dilemma. He explains:

I was a math professor, trying to teach calculus and earn my living being a math professor, but spending all my time doing computer animations at the University of Georgia, then at Carnegie Mellon, and then Case Western Reserve. But by the time I came to Carnegie Mellon, I was really spending all my time on computer graphics. They give tenure in mathematics for publishing papers on mathematics, not for doing computer animated films. (personal interview, 1 August 1988)

The solution was to find a nonacademic research position. In 1977, with the aid of pioneer Kenneth Knowlton, Max was offered a position with Lawrence Livermore Laboratories, which was seeking a researcher in computer graphics and computer animation. Max's first project at Livermore was a series of animations on molecules. They included *DNA With Ethidium*, and *Doxorubicin/DNA*. He comments on this transition:

I got into molecules because I had finished my sphere film in 1976, when I was at Case, and I was looking around for some new data. In the Micromolecular Science Department, there was a guy who was studying how drugs interact with DNA. We had done some simulations together and before I had time to do the movie, I left. So I took the data with me to Livermore and that was the first movie I did there. (personal interview, 1 August 1988)

Max was on leave from Lawrence Livermore to work on an Omni-max stereo film for Expo '90 in Japan. Upon completion of that project he returned to Lawrence Livermore.

PHILLIP MITTELMAN/MAGI

Phillip Mittelman was educated as a nuclear physicist. He received a bachelor's degree from Rensselaer Polytech Institute (RPI) and his master's degree from Harvard; he then returned to RPI to teach and complete his Ph.D. Upon completion of this degree, his first position in the nuclear industry was with Nuclear Development Associates, which, after a series of mergers, became United Nuclear Corporation (UNC).

Leaving UNC in 1966, Mittelman formed his own company, Mathematical Applications Group Inc. (MAGI), located in Elmsford, New York. He describes the types of projects they initially undertook:

> In the nuclear industry, in the particular area I worked with, which was radiation transport, we had tons of government contracts to develop some very powerful mathematical tools for tracing neutrons and gamma rays around through space. Our typical problem was: you have a reactor here and a man a couple hundred feet away, how much radiation comes to his eyes, or if a nuclear weapon goes off, how much radiation do you get in certain places. (personal interview, 11 May 1988)

The result of MAGI's research was the development of a powerful computer program coined the "Monte Carlo Radiation Transport Program." This program described a three-dimensional world in which the researcher could trace the radiation with no threat of danger (Mittelman, personal interview, 11 May 1988).

However, Mittelman soon saw the possibilities this methodology offered in other areas. He explains:

> What became clear to me, [was] that instead of tracing nuclear radiation, if we trace light, we would be able to make pictures, simulated photography. You'd trace the light, the light source to the object, to the lens of the camera. (personal interview, 11 May 1988)

In 1967 MAGI made its first computer graphic images and embarked upon a different path by establishing the first commercial computer graphics and animation production house. In 1971 MAGI released its first demonstration (demo) reel, approximately a year after its initial commercial advertising undertaking (the office equipment promotion for IBM).

The 1982 Disney production *TRON* employed 15 minutes and 235 scenes of computer generated images. It continues to maintain the record for the film containing the greatest amount of computer animation (Wilson 1986, 21). *TRON* was the product of the joint efforts of four computer animation production houses: MAGI, Triple I, Digital Effects, and Robert Abel and Associates. Mittelman recalls the initial arrangements:

> *TRON* had a lot of computer animation in it. There were two companies that they picked to do the majority of the work; MAGI and a company called Triple I, which is no longer around, but Demos and Whitney [Jr.] were there. So they were going to do the majority, about ten minutes; we were going to do about five minutes of the film. But Demos and Whitney left [Triple I] and the hardware was awkward. So we ended up doing ten minutes and they wound up doing five minutes.
>
> Abel did a little piece and a few other people did little segments, but we did most of it. (personal interview, 11 May 1988)

MAGI's approach to the production of computer graphic images was very different to others in the field. Mittelman explains:

> Their whole technology was based on representing things with polygons, and it was an analytic approach. We were representing things as three-dimensional solids and we used ray tracing. (personal interview, 11 May 1988)

After *TRON,* in anticipation of its grand success, MAGI attempted to expand, by opening an office in Los Angeles. However, *TRON* was not a commercial success and MAGI ended up not only closing the Los Angeles office, but subsequently selling to Bidmax, a Canadian company.

Mittelman then proceeded to head the UCLA Laboratory for Technology and the Arts. He described that position as

> introducing technology into the fine arts area. My function here is to help the faculty and the students move into the technology associated with the arts. (personal interview, 11 May 1988)

ROBERT ABEL/ROBERT ABEL & ASSOCIATES

Robert Abel was born in the Midwest, and raised in Shorewood, Wisconsin until the age of eleven, when his family moved to the Los

Angeles area, very close to MGM studios (David Chell 1985, 229). As a result, his introduction to filmmaking and Hollywood came early.

In his senior year in high school, Abel met producer Saul Bass, who gave him a job pasting up film titles. Bass eventually introduced Abel to John Whitney, Sr., which resulted in an introduction to computerized equipment, for the film titles were shot on Whitney's computerized analog camera device. The young Abel soon became a cameraman for Whitney.

Abel went on to enter UCLA's engineering college, but after two weeks changed his major to art (Robert Abel, telephone interview, 9 May 1988), in which he received both B.A. and M.A. degrees.

In 1963, after finishing a long project for Whitney and Saul Bass, Abel met Con Pederson, also a UCLA graduate. Pederson, who was four years Abel's senior, was a legend, for he had been hired by Disney directly upon graduation, and during World War II had worked on the space program with Werner Von Braun. Pederson offered Abel an opportunity to work on films for the World's Fair. Abel recalls:

> He [Pederson] said "I've got some World's Fair projects that I think would be good for you to work on. He showed them to me. I started working for him and we worked on a series of World's Fair projects. One he directed, which I thought was brilliant, was called *To the Moon and Beyond*." [Director Stanley] Kubrick saw the film and wanted to hire the whole office to work on *2001* for a year. I worked for Con prior to *2001* for about a year. Although we had worked on a lot of the concepts for the design of the effects for *2001*, I decided I didn't want to go to England. (telephone interview, 9 May 1988)

At this point Abel began doing documentary films and rock and roll films. He toured with Elvis Presley, Creedence Clearwater Revival, Joe Cocker, and Leon Russell (telephone interview, 9 May 1988).

In 1971, while recovering from a six-month tour with Joe Cocker and Leon Russell, Abel contacted Pederson, who was recovering from three years of work on *2001*. They agreed to rebuild the *2001* camera system and start doing some commercial work. Abel describes that period:

> We started running a slit scan and streak camera system out in the valley behind a CPA's office—no address, no telephone, no stationery. (Chell 1985, 230)

We worked on the Darwinian principle of natural selection, that the fittest clients would survive some sort of screening process and find us, despite the fact we were unlisted.

We had a couple of projects we were working on for ABC and one for Whirlpool, which was the first commercial job we ever did. (telephone interview, 9 May 1988)

This sheltered work existence lasted until 1974 when they received a contract to do a commercial for 7-Up. Abel recalls:

We got this contract to do this 7-Up commercial, and that kind of changed our lives as commercial filmmakers. We threw everything but the kitchen sink in there. We had slit scan and pure animation and multiplane animation and street photography and another technique we invented called candy apple neon and live action. (telephone interview, 9 May 1988)

The lack of hesitation and the ingenuity to combine techniques became Abel's overriding strength. Jankel and Morton maintain that Abel's main strength is in his combination of different media (1984, 126).
Abel claims his entry into computer animation was by accident.

I got into computer animation because I was interested in using computers to simulate a three-dimensional reality for certain kinds of special effects shots I was doing, particularly those that involved miniatures. Because they were very complex and if you could plan them out in advance, you could show a client. I never planned to get into computer graphics, which I thought was something Bell Labs did or JPL. I think technocracy or the technocratic elite scared me off from doing it. (Robert Abel, telephone interview, 9 May 1988)

In 1979 Disney approached Abel to produce a promotion for their new film *The Black Hole*. The result was a contract to create the title, advertising, and poster (Chell 1985, 231). This project became the predecessor or warm-up exercise for *TRON*.
In 1986 Robert Abel and Associates was sold to the Canadian company Omnibus, who had also purchased Digital Productions in a hostile takeover. In April of 1987, Omnibus went out of business, taking with it what had been two major computer animation production houses: Robert Abel and Associates, and Digital Productions.
In February of 1987, Wavefront (a company started by a former Abel art director, Bill Kovacs) purchased Robert Abel's software.

Kovacs had been head of research and development for Abel before forming his own software company in 1984.

Robert Abel is presently consulting with Apple computers and working with the development of CDI and CD ROM. Speaking of his current involvements he stated:

> I occasionally have been working in computer graphics, but I'm working in a lot of other areas related to computers. I'm particularly fascinated by the development of CDI and CD ROM, and I'm doing a lot of consultant work with Apple. (telephone interview, 9 May 1988)

Robert Abel and Associates was truly a legendary company. The unique look of its work was the product of the expectations and the fulfillment of those expectations by the individuals who labored for a common goal: the conceptualization and realization of exceptional design. As explained by Bill Kovacs:

> The one thing that was definitely true about Abel's is that the look, the design, was always primary! Technology was used, and Abel bent over backwards to hype the technology, but when it came down to the process of the commercial, the look, the feel, the design of it was king. No one there would accept a piece just because it was a novel use of fractals. It was always a *design* focus. (personal interview, 15 January 1988)

The products of this design focus (including "High Fidelity," the sexy robot in *Brilliance* and the lead-in to Steven Spielberg's *Amazing Stories*) are testimonies to Abel and his associates' dedication to the creation of unique images. These images command attention and communicate vigorously.

JUDSON ROSEBUSH/DIGITAL EFFECTS

Judson Rosebush grew up on a farm in rural Ohio. As the son of a professional educator, he was expected to attend college. He entered Syracuse University under the misconception that he could study radio; instead, he ended up receiving a master's degree in television production. However, he did become involved in radio, and ended up financing his college education by working in commercial radio (Judson Rosebush, personal interview, 5 August 1988).

Rosebush was introduced to computer animation while in graduate school at Syracuse. He viewed a film by another Syracuse graduate student in electrical engineering, Woody Anderson. He recalls:

From *Brilliance*. Robert Abel.

Woody Anderson and Dr. Donald Weiner had designed and built this language, the name of which was CALD. Computer Animated Line Drawing is what it was called, and it was able to do 2-D or 3-D computer graphics, using command-oriented language. You could make still and moving pictures this way, and this fascinated me and I began working with it, and started doing some experimental works. (Peter Sorensen 1984, 1-2)

Rosebush finished his first computer animation project, "Calderize," using CALD in 1970 (personal interview, 5 August 1988). In 1972 he made his first commercial film *Arrhythmia Monitoring*, for a company in Syracuse called Instruments for Cardiac Research. It contained two minutes of computer animation illustrating heart beats (Sorensen 1984, 2). During the next few years he produced several experimental films in which he employed optical printing techniques. However, he began to feel restricted by the CALD language and therefore began to develop his own graphic system, using the computer language Fortran.

In 1978, the computer graphics production company Digital Effects was incorporated. The seven founding partners—Judson Rosebush, Moses Weitzman, Don Leach, David Cox, Jan Prins, Jeffrey Kleiser, and Vance Leon—established headquarters in New York City (Rosebush 1984, 1-2). They specialized in both print and film media. Jankel and Morton noted:

> Digital Effects Inc., based in New York and now Los Angeles, has grown fast. Their Dicomed 48 film recorder lead to feature film quality 35mm images. Unusually, they have also made an impact in print advertising. The pointillist image of the Brooklyn Bridge for Harris Computers was an early example; the mysterious landscape image for Glaxo Inc. is more recent. (1984, 130)

Digital Effects became one of the pioneer computer animation production houses in the country. Its computer animation accomplishments include: CBS's 1979 NBA Playoffs' Opening, CBS's 1978 Sports Spectacular, *TRON*, CBS's *Universe* show opening, the *NBC Nightly News* opening, and many more.

INFORMATION INTERNATIONAL, INC. (TRIPLE I)

Triple I, founded in the early 1970s, was responsible for much of the computer-generated images seen by the public during the introductory period. Many claim it defined the state of the art of computer animation. Turner Whitted explains:

> Triple I defined the state of the art, it was mainly a place that made really glitzy stuff, but it was the first time anybody had been able to make anything quite that glitzy. . . . They formed the model for all of these production houses that spun off. It excited a lot of people . . . and showed the way for other companies. (personal interview, 1 August 1988)

Triple I utilized the talents of not only Gary Demos and John Whitney Jr., but also employed Frank Crow and James Blinn, who both served as consultants at various times, as well as effects designer and art director, Richard Taylor. It brought together some of the best talents in computer animation.

Triple I was responsible for the computer animation used in the feature films *Futureworld*, *Westworld*, and *LOOKER*, as well as parts of *TRON*. Richard Taylor, who designed the effects for *LOOKER*, explains:

> Triple I was really one of the leaders early in the business of doing raster images that were starting to get pretty amazing. They were one of the

few companies that had a film recorder that you could do that kind of imagery at high resolution on motion picture film. A lot of other people could do raster graphics, but the product had to be on TV. (personal interview, 2 August 1988)

In 1982, however, the management decided to cease work in computer animation (Thalmann and Thalmann 1985, 36). Many speculated that this was the result of their disappointment in the film industry's reaction to *TRON*. Robert Abel asserted:

I think the problem there [at Triple I] was that Whitney and Demos were really committed to making film, but Al Fanati, who owned the company, was an engineer. And I think he really expected that after *TRON* the world would beat a path to his door and he would be the Charles Lindbergh of computer animation. (telephone interview, 9 May 1988)

However, others such as Turner Whitted of Numerical Design Ltd. (NDL) posit that the motion picture division of Triple I was already in trouble before *TRON* was completed:

Disagreements among people—that's what shut down the motion picture project at Triple I. The motion picture project was an experiment. It was falling apart when *TRON* was being made. (Turner Whitted, personal interview, 1 August 1988)

Triple I, like Digital Productions and Robert Abel and Associates, was purchased by Omnibus, which went out of business in April of 1987.

CIC AND GENERAL ELECTRIC

Computer Image Corporation (CIC) and General Electric are two additional companies that played limited roles during this introductory period. The two companies, although both prominent at this time, had very different goals: CIC was a computer graphics and animation commercial production house, while General Electric was a division of a major corporation which focused on simulation design.

CIC, located in Denver, Colorado, began producing computer graphics commercials in 1969 (Frank Crow, personal interview, 16 May 1988). Their system CAESAR (Computer Animated Episodes using Single Axis Rotation) was an analog computer graphics system (Jankel and Morton 1984, 125).

General Electric's contribution focused on real time simulation, specifically flight simulators. Judson Rosebush explains:

> General Electric, in Syracuse, built the first real-time full-color interactive system—a flight simulator for NASA's manned space program. This simulator was completed in 1967. (1979, 21)

This system became the prototype for future training simulators manufactured by Evans and Sutherland and other flight simulator manufacturers.

The companies which emerged during this introductory period shared one very evident goal: a strong focus on design. The concentration on innovation, composition, form, and execution became the focal point of each production, for each company. The pursuit of this goal appeared to be an unspoken rule for the pioneer players. Judson Rosebush asserts:

> The first-generation companies replaced a set of companies who are computerized motion control companies. Those companies, as well as the first-generation computer animation companies, all have a strong design focus. They all very much specialize in selling design, conceptualization and path-finding design is very much a signature of these places. (personal interview, 5 August 1988)

Each company had its own specialized and distinguishable "look" and continued to somehow maintain that "look" while at the same time pressing ahead, challenging the newly completed and pursuing the next visual revelation.

6

The Second Wave

The second wave, or second-generation computer animation houses as Judson Rosebush termed them (personal interview, 5 August 1988), includes: Pacific Data Images (PDI), established in 1980 by Carl Rosendahl; Cranston-Csuri, established by Charles Csuri, Robert Kanuth, and James Kristoff in 1981; Lucasfilm's computer animation division, which emerged in 1980 from the efforts of Ed Catmull and Alvy Ray Smith and later became Pixar; and Digital Productions, which was founded in 1981 by John Whitney Jr. and Gary Demos. These production houses, like their predecessors, focused on design and the fabrication of unique images. Some, such as Pixar and Cranston-Csuri, also designed software tools and fabricated and built hardware equipment.

PACIFIC DATA IMAGES (PDI)/CARL ROSENDAHL

Carl Rosendahl grew up in the Los Angeles area, where he was exposed to filmmaking in high school. This, he claims, is where he "got the bug to be in the film and television industry" (personal interview, 21 December 1988). After receiving his bachelor's degree in electrical engineering from Stanford University, he worked in reverse engineering for nine months. Reverse engineering of computers is, as he describes it,

> where you take them apart under a microscope and see how they work for the competition. (personal interview, 21 December 1988)

He left reverse engineering and did research and design for Memorex until his research group was dissolved. At this point he decided

> to do computer graphics, I wanted to be involved in the entertainment industry, television, and film or music. Computer graphics seemed like a

real good junction for what I wanted to do. It's very technical and at the same time, very artistic. It was for a guy with a degree in engineering, electrical engineering. Computer science was basically the same thing at that point. (personal interview, 21 December 1988)

In 1980, as a result of his desire to do computer graphics and be involved in the entertainment industry, Rosendahl founded Pacific Data Images (PDI). In 1982 he hired two partners, Glenn Entis and Richard Chuang, and negotiated a research and development contract with Global Television in Brazil. This provided PDI's investment capital. Rosendahl elaborates:

What they wanted in Brazil was the ability to do computer animation in-house for their station ID's and openings. They wanted that and we wanted money and larger computers. So we struck a deal with them. They gave us a VAX computer and quite a bit of money. We got the VAX to use for a year. At the end of that point of time, we gave them a subset of the software we developed for them to use in Brazil. That's basically what acted as our equivalent to venture capital. We needed the money, and the fortunate thing about us is that we didn't have to give up any equity and to this day we remain the only three stockholders. (personal interview, 21 December 1988)

PDI is considered one of the most, if not *the* most, successful computer animation production house. Many claim this success was due to their approach to slow, incremental growth. Turner Whitted agrees:

PDI seems to lead a charmed existence, and a lot of that is because they did not start off in a grandiose style, they started off small. They paid as they went, they stuck to their knitting in doing just one type of thing well. They've established a look. They started off with three guys and now there are 30 and they've done it over a period of six years. And that's about right. (personal interview, 1 August 1988)

Another reason for PDI's stability and success is their choice of equipment; as with their outlook on expansion, they make their choices cautiously, with great prudence and a lack of extravagance. Rosendahl defined their approach:

The approach we took is to have a large number of smaller machines, so that it's easy to turn them over. When they start going out of date, that's fine, you throw them away and start buying new ones. When one breaks,

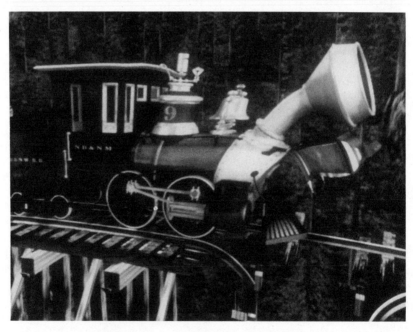

Frames from *Locomotion*. Pacific Data Images.

you're not out of business, you're limping a little. (personal interview, 21 December 1988)

PDI's eminent presence has influenced the kinds of images which appear in television graphics. They are major contributors to the impact that computer animation has made on the broadcast industry. However, they are now beginning to pursue additional avenues in advertising, television programs, motion pictures, and educational video. One example of this expansion is the computer-animated puppet they produced for the *Jim Henson Hour,* which aired in January 1989 (Carl Rosendahl, personal interview, 21 December 1988). Rosendahl discussed the direction they are taking:

The long-term direction for us is getting into what I call long-format animation, which is anything over a minute, but more realistically for television programs, motion pictures, educational videos. We're focusing mostly on the television industry. It's the goal we've chosen. (personal interview, 21 December 1988)

CRANSTON-CSURI

Cranston-Csuri was the realization of Charles Csuri's conceptual dream. In 1981 Charles Csuri approached entrepreneur Robert Cranston Kanuth with an idea:

at the time I thought there was an opportunity to one, make money and [two] to do some things that were interesting. (Charles Csuri, personal interview, 18 November 1987)

Kanuth consulted his business partner James Kristoff, former treasurer of Ohio State University, who recalled:

My partner, Bob Kanuth, whose middle name is Cranston, received this idea from Chuck Csuri. He [Csuri] thought there was some commercial application of computer animation. So he approached Bob Kanuth and said he needed money and business expertise. So Bob asked me to look into it. (personal interview, 27 January 1988)

After Kristoff researched the issue, he advised Kanuth to proceed. The result was the 1981 establishment of Cranston-Csuri Productions, with Kanuth as the chairman, Kristoff as the president, and Csuri as the executive vice president. At first, both Kristoff and Csuri maintained half-time status with their employers; however, in September of 1982, the company took its first job, and Kristoff's status changed to full time. Csuri, on the other hand, continued his half-time position with Ohio State University.

> I cut back on my university commitment to 50 percent [of the] time, and in the first few years I worked in the capacity of the company, putting together the talent, and the software to get it going, and helped establish the standards of quality. (Charles Csuri, personal interview, 18 November 1987)

Csuri hired some of his graduate students to write software and conduct test animations. Michael Collery, who is presently at PDI, was one of the graduate research associates hired. He recalls:

> At that time we were trying to get enough animation together to put together a demo reel. It was an ideal situation, where all I had to do was think about animation and produce it, no client to please. (personal interview, 13 May 1988)

Cranston-Csuri Productions became known for their mirrored and translucent images, their reflective surfaces, and their graceful glasslike bouncing balls.

However, the foundation of these elegant images was experiencing great turbulence. The management and the governing board were at odds over two issues which focused on the direction of the company. Csuri felt the narrow commercial broadcast focus was very short-sighted and that there was a pressing need to embrace other types of projects and abandon expensive and time-consuming custom animation.

> I got disenchanted with the direction of the company because I felt that commercial broadcast television was not the way to go, [nor was] custom animation. We had to get into some other kinds of projects, maybe closer to simulation and training, or medical. (Charles Csuri, personal interview, 18 November 1987)

Kristoff also felt there was an urgent need for a change in direction, but his focus was on expansion. He perceived the need to establish an office in Los Angeles, in order to attract the broadcast and film clientele who were reluctant to venture to Ohio.

We were having difficulty in attracting clients to Columbus, even from New York and Cleveland. They wanted to go to Los Angeles. There's a feeling in the marketplace that you are second-rate if you weren't in New York or Los Angeles. (James Kristoff, personal interview, 27 January 1988)

Csuri's position created a conflict between himself, the board, and the management of the company. Consequently, he decided to "simply back away" (Charles Csuri, personal interview, 18 November 1988). Kristoff, however, pursued his path by organizing a series of investment proposals, including an attempt to purchase Cranston-Csuri. However, each of three separate offerings systematically fell through. The end result was his resignation from Cranston-Csuri and his subsequent establishment of Metrolight Studios in Los Angeles.

I came out here in October and hired some of the people that had just been laid off at Cranston-Csuri, and some other people that had been at Digital Productions and Abel, and [I] started Metrolight Studios. (James Kristoff, personal interview, 27 January 1988)

At this point, the management decided to liquidate Cranston-Csuri Productions, and, as of October 1987, Cranston-Csuri went out of business.

LUCASFILM/PIXAR

Pixar, an offshoot or spin-off of Lucasfilm, emerged in 1986. The individuals involved—Ed Catmull, Alvy Ray Smith, and David DeFrancisco—can be traced back to NYIT [New York Institute of Technology], where they all began in 1974. During that period at NYIT, Catmull designed the Computer-Assisted Animation System (CAAS), and the animation program "TWEEN," and Smith developed the paint system, "PAINT" (Thalmann and Thalmann 1985, 35).

In 1979 Catmull was contacted by Lucasfilm, which resulted in an interview trip for Smith and himself. In July 1979, Catmull was hired by Lucasfilm to identify film production areas which could be aided by computer equipment.

I examined what they were doing with video editing, digital audio, and computer graphics. (Ed Catmull, personal interview, 19 May 1988)

Three equipment components were suggested:

> One of them was a digital film printer; the second thing was a digital
> audio synthesizer, and the third thing was a computer controlled digital
> editor. (Alvy Ray Smith, personal interview, 19 May 1988)

Alvy Ray Smith was hired six months later. However, at first there
was a great deal of hesitancy at Lucasfilm about investing money in
a computer division; the success of *The Empire Strikes Back* eased
that concern.

> They weren't really willing to spend a substantial amount of money until
> it was apparent to them that *The Empire Strikes Back* was going to be
> successful. Then they decided to invest money in a computer division. At
> that point we brought in Ralph Guggenheim to head up video editing,
> and Andy Moorer to do digital audio. At that time we began to form the
> computer graphics group. (Ed Catmull, personal interview, 19 May 1988)

With the finance issue resolved, Catmull and Smith proceeded to
establish a group of individuals who could serve both causes: design
the equipment requested by Lucas and also contribute to a computer
graphics effort.

> We started putting the team together to execute these three machines that
> we were to build, but at the same time, we were putting together a
> computer graphics group. (Alvy Ray Smith, personal interview, 19 May
> 1988)

This group consisted of Ed Catmull, Alvy Ray Smith (who headed
the computer graphics effort), David DeFrancisco (who designed the
digital film printer), Andy Moorer from Stanford (who headed the
digital audio project), and Ralph Guggenheim (who directed the
video editor effort).

The climate at Lucasfilm toward computer graphics, however, was
not as accepting as Catmull and Smith had anticipated.

> It became pretty clear fairly early on, that there wasn't a lot of enthusiasm
> that we thought there would be inside Lucasfilm for computer graphics.
> (Alvy Ray Smith, personal interview, 19 May 1988)

However, in 1981, Industrial Light and Magic (ILM), the special
effects unit of Lucasfilm, was assigned a sequence in *Star Trek II, The
Wrath of Khan,* which baffled them. So they approached the computer

graphics group with their visual problem, a sixty-second sequence in which:

> They wanted to show early in the movie what the genesis effect was, some kind of demonstration of what it means to turn death into life. (Alvy Ray Smith, personal interview, 19 May 1988)

Smith immediately called together his graphics group and planned a strategy. He proposed to

> make a TV commercial for Lucasfilm about what computer graphics means. . . . I had just come from JPL and the Voyager flyby had just happened on one of the planets, so I suggested 'why don't we have a flyby of a dead moonlit planet?'

> Bill Reeves came in and said he'd make a fire. This projectile will impact the planet with the genesis effect and it will explode. Fire will spread all over the planet and fractals will grow out of melted surfaces and it will turn into Earth and then it will fly away. (personal interview, 19 May 1988)

Loren Carpenter, who had been hired earlier that year, was a specialist in fractals, so he immediately undertook creating fractal mountains and oceans for the sequence. He also was responsible for designing the complex camera move which Smith suggested. He recalls:

> This was our first real project. The first time we'd taken all these tools that we'd developed and tried to use them for something bigger than a test case. (personal interview, 19 May 1988)

The special effects which were used in *Star Trek II* were also demonstrations of software and hardware equipment developed at Lucasfilm. One example is William Reeves's "Particle System":

> Reeves has produced a method for modeling fuzzy objects such as fire, clouds, and water. The technique, called "Particle Systems" was used in the Genesis Demo sequence from the movie *Star Trek II* and for the explosion caused by the destruction of the Death Star's power generator in *Return of the Jedi*. (Thalmann and Thalmann 1985, 36)

Alvy Ray Smith confirms this observation and explains the rationale:

> Every time we do an animation, since it's not our business, we do it to demonstrate a new technique that has never been mastered before.

Genesis demo showed fractals for the first time and particle systems, and a tiny bit of motion blur. (personal interview, 19 May 1988)

In 1984, John Lasseter joined the Lucasfilm computer graphics group. His first contribution was a computer-generated character animation entitled *The Adventures of Andre & Wally B.* Alvy Ray Smith directed it and Bill Reeves, Rob Cook, Ed Catmull, and Loren Carpenter all worked on assorted technical aspects. Smith defined each member's contribution in the manner of a jazz quartet leader; "We had Loren on fractals, Rob Cook on texture maps, and Bill Reeves on particle systems" (personal interview, 19 May 1988). Loren Carpenter remembers:

> About that time we picked up John Lasseter from Disney, who had just finished a project there. He and Alvy and the rest of us made up this little story about this character Andre and Wally B. Mostly it was John who was responsible for the story and the characters.

> Ed Catmull wrote the program that defined the surface that's used for Andre's body. You see a pear shape that bends . . . It's called a teardrop. That's the name we gave to it. We've used it a lot in other things. (personal interview, 22 January 1988)

The Adventures of Andre & Wally B. once again demonstrated new techniques developed at Lucasfilm, the "teardrop" and motion blur. Carpenter explains:

> That film was the first computer-animated film to have motion blur and also the first to attempt character animation with 3-D characters. (personal interview, 22 January 1988)

In 1985, discussions and negotiations had already begun for the computer graphics group to split from Lucasfilm. There was a concern that Lucasfilm had branched out into too many areas and needed to once again focus on filmmaking (Ed Catmull, personal interview, 19 May 1988). The last film the computer graphics group worked on as part of Lucasfilm was a Spielberg umbrella production called *Young Sherlock Holmes*.

On 5 February 1986 the computer graphics group of Lucasfilm officially became its own company, Pixar. The video and audio groups had already departed from Lucasfilm and combined efforts to establish Droidworks.

Three computer animations have been produced by Pixar since its inception: the international award winner and 1986 Academy Award nominee *Luxo Jr.; Red's Dream;* and the 1989 Academy Award winner for best animated short film, *Tin Toy. Luxo Jr.* illustrated Pixar's technical advances in

> articulated self-shadowing, self-shadowing by articulated objects. It also showed off distributed light sources in the frame itself. (Alvy Ray Smith, personal interview, 19 May 1988)

Loren Carpenter describes *Red's Dream* as

> a movie that had two phases in it. . . . Some of it would be gritty reality and another would be fantasy, in a different world. (22 January 1988)

Red's Dream demonstrated extreme complexity; the bike shop scene alone had thirty million polygons per frame (Alvy Ray Smith, personal interview, 19 May 1988).

Pixar has two goals, as Loren Carpenter defined them:

> Our primary mission is visualization. We see it as taking data in the form of geometry or real world samples of process or simulations from supercomputers and transforming that data, using our computer graphics technology and our image processing technology into images that people can use. So we see ourselves as heading that in every way possible, by providing rendering machines and image computers that will turn volumes of images and raw data into raster images.

> As far as animation is concerned, we want to continue to push the state of the art of animation for several reasons. It gives us good press, it attracts good people, and it pushes our ability to manage that kind of imagery. (personal interview, 22 January 1988)

In April 1989, Pixar's *Tin Toy* became the first computer animation to win an Academy Award. John Lasseter and Bill Reeves were the proud recipients. This was a clear statement from the film industry that computer animation is indeed a respected film genre and does have the potential to hold a highly regarded position in this medium.

EDWIN CATMULL

Ed Catmull grew up in Salt Lake City, Utah. From his earliest days of recollection, Catmull planned to be an animator. However, his lack of drawing abilities became clear as he entered college, directing him towards physics. At the University of Utah he majored in physics and computer science. After graduating in 1969, he worked for a limited time before returning to the University of Utah and entering the computer science graduate program. Pioneer Ivan Sutherland and David Evans both served on his dissertation committee.

Catmull's very first project was an animated hand. He describes it:

> I took a class, and the interesting thing about the class was that they already had a canned set of routines if you wanted to make animated films. There were only two people in the class who didn't use canned routines, but instead chose to write something ourselves. I did the hand and Fred Parke did the face. We combined the two films together and showed them in Boston in 1972. (personal interview, 19 May 1988)

Catmull's contributions to computer animation include curved surfaces, texture mapping, and the Z buffer. He explains:

> I was working on curved surfaces. In doing curved surfaces, I invented the Z buffer. I did the display of curved surfaces, which at the time I thought was the most important thing I did. But in fact, the texture mapping that I developed had a greater effect. (personal interview, 19 May 1988)

After graduation, Catmull spent a short time at Applicon, where he got a call from Alex Schure's secretary. He recalls:

> I got a call from Alex Schure's secretary arranging for my airfare down to New York. I had no idea who the woman was or why she was trying to get me to New York. I was asked to go down to New York Institute of Technology, to talk with Alex Schure. Alex wanted to set up a computer animation lab. He offered me to come and head it up. So, I accepted. (personal interview, 19 May 1988)

In November 1974, Catmull set up shop in the estate garage structure on NYIT's campus. Within six months, Catmull received a call from Alvy Ray Smith, who had been advised by Martin Newell of the University of Utah, to contact Catmull. After a meeting with Schure and Catmull, Smith was hired at NYIT.

During their reign at NYIT, Catmull designed his animation program, TWEEN, and Smith designed his paint program, PAINT. This was the beginning of a very long collaborative relationship, which has spanned more than fifteen years.

In 1979 a call from Lucasfilm resulted in Catmull's departure from NYIT and the beginning of establishing steps towards the creation of a computer graphics group at Lucasfilm. By early 1980, Smith had been hired by Lucasfilm and the Catmull-Smith team was reunited. They began efforts to assemble some of the most creative and talented individuals in digital device design and computer graphics. The result was the creation of one of the strongest computer graphics groups in the industry.

Catmull had been at Lucasfilm for four years when, in 1985, he began negotiations with Lucasfilm for the computer graphics group to spin out and become its own entity. It was a long and difficult process which took about a year. He explains the reason for the delay:

> It was a long, hard process to go through because of the changes Lucasfilm was going through. We did a number of things to get financing, but unfortunately Lucasfilm was asking a lot of money for the division to be bought out, and that's what took so long. (personal interview, 19 May 1988)

Negotiations were completed in 1986 and Ed Catmull became the president of the newly formed Pixar. He states:

> We're not a public company. Essentially all the assets in this company are the people. So if you don't make the people happy, you lose the assets. It had to be a good deal for everybody involved. (personal interview, 19 May 1988)

ALVY RAY SMITH

Alvy Ray Smith was born in Mineral Wells, Texas and raised in New Mexico. He produced his first computer image when he was a student at New Mexico State University. He recalls:

> I did my first computer picture when I was in college in New Mexico State University. I was working in the antenna laboratory. The head engineer came to me and said "Alvy, I want you to plot this spiral, this antenna design for this weather satellite." I had just taken a computer class and thought, "I bet a computer can do that." I went over to the computer center and whipped one out. That was my first computer graphic. That was in 1964. (personal interview, 19 May 1988)

After accidently discovering Marvin Minsky's article, "Steps Towards Artificial Intelligence," Smith developed a new interest to pursue.

I was totally captivated by the idea. There were two places in the world that had it, one was MIT where Minsky was, and Stanford. I applied to both places and got accepted by both places, but I got a scholarship to Stanford, and that's where I went. (personal interview, 19 May 1988)

Smith received his Ph.D. from Stanford in 1968 and was hired by New York University to teach cellular automata.

During that stint at NYU I was doing cellular automata. That's what I did my thesis on, self-reproducing machines. It's the mathematics of parallel computers. (Alvy Ray Smith, personal interview, 19 May 1988)

While at NYU, he published several papers on cellular automata and designed a drawing, which has served as the cover of *Foundations of Computer Science Journal* for the past fifteen years. These events in his life he refers to as his "pre-computer graphics period."

In 1973, Smith broke his leg and was in a full-body cast for three months. Literally helpless, he spent this time reevaluating his situation:

I just sat there and thought about everything. I'm doing the wrong thing in life. I have this artistic talent. I've been known for drawing pictures all my life and I'm not doing anything with it.

I was a professor of computer science, but my soul has always been art based. (personal interview, 19 May 1988)

In 1974 Smith moved to Berkeley to teach cellular automata theory at the University of California. While there, he decided to contact a friend, Richard Shoup, who was designing a computer paint program at Xerox PARC. Enthusiastically embracing Shoup's device and the artistic possibilities it offered, Smith immediately began creating images. This soon led to his securing a position with Xerox PARC. Describing his duties, he stated:

My role was to show off Dick's [Shoup] machine, to make art on it, make videotapes on it, show it to people so they'd know what it was. (personal interview, 19 May 1988)

His first major project was a videotape entitled "Vidbits." This, he declares, is "when I got turned on to computer graphics in a big way." However, after he had been there only a few months, Xerox decided it did not want to pursue color, and that its focus was to be black-and-white office systems.

During this time Smith also met an artist, David DeFrancisco, with whom he worked very closely at Xerox PARC. Prior to Xerox's decision to change focus, Smith and DeFrancisco applied jointly for an NEA grant.

They received the grant, but by that time they had no facility in which to work. They visited the University of Utah and met with Martin Newell who referred them to Ed Catmull (who was at that time at New York Institute of Technology). Smith and DeFrancisco met with Schure, Catmull, and Malcolm Blanchard, and were hired to work on Schure's computer-animated feature-length film effort. Smith says of Schure:

> He was doing a feature-length movie. He was serious about it and he was also serious about using computers. He knew before anybody else—he was willing to step out and put money on the line that computers and pictures were going to go together somehow. He did it. He was the courageous guy who stepped out there and made a commitment before anybody else. (personal interview, 19 May 1988)

Through Schure's financial sources, Catmull, Smith, and DeFrancisco were able to assemble one of, if not *the* most, state-of-the-art computer graphics laboratories in the nation. They purchased the first commercial frame buffer from Evans and Sutherland and the first VAX computer. The equipment, purchased in conjunction with the programs designed by Catmull and Smith, provided NYIT with the most sophisticated facilities in the world.

Unfortunately, facilities and talents are not always all that it takes. Schure's direction ended up bringing the downfall of this computer animation utopia; the project he envisioned had no real substance. But the real strength of that institution lay in its technical staff, as Catmull explains:

> The creative capability was in the technical staff of the computer group, where we had the best computer research group in the world. (personal interview, 19 May 1988)

In 1979, after four years at NYIT, Smith and Catmull visited Lucasfilm, in response to a phone call Catmull received from them. The result of that visit was a master plan devised by Catmull and Smith in which Catmull would be hired and Smith and DeFrancisco would eventually be brought on. The plan worked, Catmull was indeed hired. Smith and DeFrancisco then immediately resigned from NYIT to work temporarily with JPL until Catmull could hire them at Lucasfilm. During this brief six-month period, Smith and DeFrancisco worked with James Blinn on the *Cosmos* series.

In 1980, Smith began implementing the plan to organize a computer graphics group at Lucasfilm. He ultimately became the head of the computer graphics team. In this position he directed the *Star Trek II* "Genesis Demo," and *The Adventures of Andre & Wally B.*

In February of 1986 Alvy Ray Smith became the Executive Vice President of Pixar.

LOREN CARPENTER

Loren Carpenter moved to Washington state when he was four. He went to the University of Washington in Seattle and began working for Boeing in 1968. During the thirteen years he was with Boeing, he developed a series of programming skills which he applied to computer graphics. His goal was to do computer graphics.

> I always wanted to do graphics, make pictures. I eventually worked myself into a computer-aided design group. It was the closest that Boeing had in computer graphics or computer animation. And that was the equipment that would let me make pictures of things besides airplanes. (Loren Carpenter, personal interview, 22 January 1988)

His calculated plan worked. In January of 1981, Carpenter's plan was realized; he was hired by Lucasfilm. He admits:

> It was not an accident. I went out of my way to get them to notice me. But I did it in a way that was clear that it was more than show. (personal interview, 22 January 1988)

Carpenter's role in the "Genesis Demo" was the creation of mountains and oceans which allowed him to utilize his expertise with fractals. However, he feels his strengths focus on algorithms:

> Mostly what I feel I do best around here, as far as programming, is taking and bending algorithms and turning them into working code. Once I understand how something works, then writing it into a program is about as difficult as explaining it to someone. A lot of what I do on my own is

Frame from *Vol Libre*. Loren Carpenter.

to try and figure out how things work. The talent is useful in programming things that haven't been programmed before. (personal interview, 22 January 1988)

In 1984, *The Adventures of Andre & Wally B.* sent Carpenter and Rob Cook to the Cray factory in Minnesota to work on the "motion blur" frames of the film.

The production on that film was a real bear because "motion blur" is not free and takes more computer time. These "motion blur" frames were costing us two or three times as much as the "non-blur" frames. (Loren Carpenter, personal interview, 22 January 1988)

Carpenter and Cook spent a month in Minnesota, first converting their software to run on the Cray, then producing enough of the film in order to show it at SIGGRAPH.

Loren's favorite project remains his first film, *Vol Libre*.

The favorite thing I've ever done would be my first film, *Vol Libre*. When I figured out how to do fractals, it was very simple approximations. In the space of about two minutes I'd seen the film that I was going to do. (personal interview, 22 January 1988)

Carpenter was inspired to pursue the generation of computer images by two groups of pioneers. He expounds:

> There are two levels of pioneering. The pioneers in synthetic imagery and those have to be people at Utah and Illinois. Utah, it's Watkins and Warnock. At Illinois it's Bouknight and Kelley. Those two people inspired me to think about the possibility that one could actually use a computer to make a synthetic image, not just lines. They were the people who invented the hidden surface algorithms as opposed to hidden line algorithms. (personal interview, 22 January 1988)

Carpenter's basic need "to explore new things" is his driving force. An environment like Pixar, where imagination, intrigue, persistence, and talent are fundamental tools, is indeed an appropriate place for Loren Carpenter.

DIGITAL PRODUCTIONS

In 1981 John Whitney, Jr. and Gary Demos founded Digital Productions, immediately following their departure from Triple I, where they had formed the Motion Pictures Project group. This special interest group within Triple I collaborated on feature films such as the 1976 film *Futureworld,* and the 1980 production, *LOOKER.* They were to also work on *TRON;* however, disagreements concerning computing power caused Whitney, Jr. and Demos to depart from Triple I. Demos explains:

> We worked on the preparation of the film *TRON.* We were designing it to do ourselves at Triple I. At that time, we were hoping to have more computing power available . . . Unfortunately Triple I was not terribly healthy at the time, so they really didn't want to back the project. John and I actually had a fight with Triple I over the subject of computing power. . . .
>
> We did some of the tests for it and worked on the story for about two years before we left. The third part of the film was done with the technology that we developed there. (Chell 1985, 251)

The founding principle which Digital Productions centered itself upon was increased computing power. Demos elaborates:

> The original concept at Digital Productions [was] to increase computing power . . . We wanted to capitalize on what we had learned with the machines we had at Information International. (Chell 1985, 252)

This focus on computing power has affected each of the Whitney-Demos endeavors. They have consistently pursued and depended on supercomputing capabilities for their image making. However, accompanying that concentration with equal forcefulness are difficulties and disadvantages, such as the initial expense incurred by the purchase of a Cray computer or a connection machine, and the time and expense incurred when the computer is not functioning, for it brings all production to a halt. Ed Catmull, who at the time was at Lucasfilm, has paid a visit to Digital Productions to evaluate their facilities, and remarked:

> We in fact went down there just to analyze it and just to look at the economics of it. The economics did not make sense! It was too much money and could never be justified . . . I don't think a supercomputer is the way to go. The correct way to go is with the smaller computers which have become more powerful. You need to have cheap stations for each person. If you depend on the services of a supercomputer then you can never become economically viable. (personal interview, 19 May 1988)

Alvy Ray Smith, Catmull's partner for eight years at that time, accompanied him on his site visit to Digital Productions. He added:

> I've never been able to understand how these people can talk themselves into it. You can't pay for a Cray. We were at Lucasfilm, one of the wealthier film companies, and we couldn't afford a Cray. (personal interview, 19 May 1988)

The Cray computer is one of the most expensive pieces of equipment the industry offers, bringing up a major issue which leaders in the computer animation production industry focus on: the cost-effectiveness of such an investment. Carl Rosendahl of PDI voices two additional elements:

> Digital Productions had a Cray—the least cost-effective piece of equipment for doing these kind of things around. The idea of using one huge machine doesn't work, because to write off a machine like that you're going to have to run it at capacity for a large number of years. And this industry, just first of all, won't support that much business right now. And secondly, all of the technology is changing way too rapidly. (personal interview, 21 December 1988)

Gary Demos, however, alleges that the difference in the equipment creates a difference in the market pursued and that this balances cost-effectiveness:

It seems to me that the market forces are different if you don't have a supercomputer, than the market forces if you do. If you do have a supercomputer and you're like us, you have a thinking machine. What you're competing against is the cost performance of what you're able to do versus other techniques. In general, we've had enough success with that, that we're able to compete effectively against live action, models, or hand animation. (personal interview, 5 May 1988)

Cynthia Goodman in her book *Digital Visions* stated that:

With the realistic simulation of the natural world as their goal, they [Digital Productions] developed this process, which requires a Cray X-MP supercomputer capable of performing 400 million mathematical calculations per second. The computational demands for the creation of realistic computer-simulated scenes are staggering. (1987, 162)

However, computer systems designer and NDL president, Turner Whitted's observation of the situation differs from Goodman's:

Digital Productions' basic premise was that it requires supercomputing horsepower to do the kind of graphics that people want. The fact is, no it doesn't require supercomputer horsepower. They had a lot of overhead. They didn't do enough commercial work to balance them, to pay the bills when the film work was slack. Everything they did was expensive, there was no way to do cheap work there. (personal interview, 1 August 1988)

Some of the projects produced by Digital Productions include: the generation of the spaceships in *The Last Starfighter,* the flying owl title sequence for Jim Henson's film *Labyrinth,* and the famous "Hard Woman" in Mick Jagger's rock video. When reviewing these productions, one fails to see a "simulation of the natural world," but rather one observes the simulation of mythical fabricated worlds.

JOHN WHITNEY, JR.

The son of a painter (his mother, Jackie) and an experimental filmmaker and pioneer computer animator (his father, John Whitney), John Whitney, Jr. was born to a most unusual family. Eugene Youngblood described eloquently the environment in which John, Jr. and his brothers, Michael and Mark, grew up:

They were raised in an environment of science, technology and the arts, Eastern philosophy. John Cage, Buckminster Fuller, and Jordon Belson have been their houseguests. Their eyes and ears have been nourished by higher orders of sight and sound than most of us are able to conceive. (1970, 128-29)

Whitney's own recollection of his childhood confirms these influences:

I grew up in a family that was making abstract films, and I was fascinated by the images that were around me while I was growing up. When I got out of high school, I had a pretty good sense in my mind about what I wanted to do. In fact, when I was fifteen, I worked with my Dad building a mechanical analog system, which we called the 'CAM' machine. That experience made a big impression on me and I started working with that system, both from a filmmaking point of view (I was using it to make my own films) and I was also building that system, which taught me a lot about how to make images using computer-like systems. (personal interview, 5 May 1988)

At eighteen, Whitney, Jr. completed his first computer film, *Byjina Flores,* in 1965. In describing the film Whitney, Jr. shares his disappointment:

My idea was to work with illusions of color and retinal persistence of images. There's one point where it only slightly works as I intended, so the film becomes a total failure for me. (Youngblood 1970, 230)

In 1967, the twenty-year-old Whitney had generated over five thousand feet of computer film, producing a sequential triptych which premiered at the 1967 Montreal Exposition. Whitney described the creative process of this project:

I became merely an instrumentality in tune with a force, a creative energy force which expressed itself. I was able to make the films without thinking too much about what I was doing. There was just this continuous flow of energy between me, the machine, and the images. But the machine became transparent. I don't think I was conscious of any systematic manipulation or exploration of a geometrical theme, though it is undeniably in the film. (Youngblood 1970, 233)

For a brief period in the mid-1970s John Whitney Jr. worked for the Picture/Design Group (P/DG) in Santa Monica, California. This company, founded by Ivan Sutherland, stayed in business for only nine months. Upon its collapse, Whitney, Jr. and Gary Demos, who had been working together at P/DG, decided to join forces and pursue computer graphics design. Whitney and Demos had met previously, during Demos' CalTech student years, when he worked with Whitney, Sr. So they approached Information International Inc. (Triple I) and proposed that they combine talents and form a new group, "The Motion Picture Project." Demos described the proposal collaboration:

> We thought that the technology they had with regard to film—exposing color film, and scanning color film, which they hadn't done yet—would be very relevant to what we wanted to do. We would bring in the technology for making simulated images and then work with them on how to get really good recording quality out of the system. (Chell 1985, 250)

Whitney looks upon this period as a major turning point in the direction of his life:

> I was in my late twenties when I had the opportunity to see my first graphic images and those experiences were pivotal in forming my career, in that I gained an insight how electronic computers could be used to make images for not just filmmaking, but I saw a path that led to special effects, motion graphics, photo product simulation of animation, and ultimately to the photo of human beings. (personal interview, 5 May 1988)

This relationship with Triple I lasted until 1981, when Whitney, Jr. and Demos departed over disagreements concerning increasing computing power. They immediately formed Digital Productions, which stayed in business until the unfriendly Omnibus takeover in 1986. Robert Abel, of Robert Abel and Associates, in discussing the Omnibus presence in computer animation production houses stated:

> In the case of Digital Productions, they were the product of an unfriendly takeover by Omnibus, which was publically held. (telephone interview, 5 May 1988)

However, once again Whitney prevailed with a new company he established solely, Digital Animation Laboratory in Hollywood, California (Whitney, telephone interview, January 1991).

GARY DEMOS

Gary Demos, like John Whitney, Jr., is a native Californian. He attended the University of Southern California and received his Ph.D.

from California Institute of Technology (CalTech). His introduction to computer graphics occurred while he was at CalTech, where he met John Whitney, Sr., who conducted an arts program there. Whitney, Sr. showed a selection of his films, which sparked Demos's interest in this medium:

> I had a great deal of interest in how the images were made and what it took to make them. I'd always been interested in music, and Whitney, Sr. was essentially doing visually what musicians do musically, so it seemed to me that it potentially could be as aesthetically rewarding and interesting to me as music had always been. (Chell 1985, 247)

Demos, along with twenty students, originally (which soon dwindled down to three), began creating computer graphics. They were also introduced to Whitney, Sr.'s optical printing system, which was located in his home. This is where Demos met John Whitney, Jr., later to become his partner.

After completing his program at CalTech, Demos's growing interest in computer graphics led him to a consulting position for an IBM film series on computers. Following the completion of that project, he began working for the Evans and Sutherland Company in Salt Lake City, Utah, which eventually led to his working directly for Ivan Sutherland. Demos described the influence Sutherland contributed to his experience in computer graphics:

> I worked for a while with Ivan Sutherland at Evans and Sutherland Company. He got me an initial orientation about what we call shaded computer graphics—the kind with surfaces. (personal interview, 5 May 1988)

Sutherland and Demos's shared interest in filmmaking brought them both to California to start a computer graphics company, Picture/Design Group in Santa Monica (Chell 1985, 248-49). The termination of P/DG prompted the first of several Whitney-Demos ventures. Their "Motion Pictures Project Group" at Triple I was the first endeavor, which lasted until 1981, and was immediately followed by the creation of Digital Productions, which endured until the 1986 Omnibus takeover. And the last venture was Whitney-Demos Productions, which immediately preceded the Digital Productions enterprise.

Throughout these undertakings there has been an underlying inspiration, which Demos described:

I suppose I'm inspired to some degree by films in general and special effects in films. When special effects are used to tell the interesting story points, that probably wouldn't be told without the special effects, I've always appreciated that. So that's what's been an inspiration to me. (personal interview, 5 May 1988)

In 1988 Whitney-Demos closed and John Whitney and Gary Demos parted. Throughout their joint undertakings the Whitney-Demos combination had been the blending of Gary Demos's technology with the design strengths of John Whitney, Jr.

RICHARD TAYLOR

Richard Taylor was born in San Antonio, Texas. The son of an air force officer, he led the early life of an "air force brat," living in Texas, New York, California, Ohio, Alaska, and Japan. However, he reveals:

We kind of called Utah home, because that's where he [my father] finally retired . . . My first two years in high school were in Alaska, and my second two were in Dayton, Ohio. (personal interview, 2 August 1988)

Columbia Prep School in Washington, D.C. immediately followed high school graduation, for although Taylor had received art scholarships to Miami, Ohio, and the University of Colorado, he was attempting to enter one of the federal academies. However, his college board scores were not high enough; nevertheless, after six months he entered Annapolis. He explains:

Even though I had been offered art scholarships and athletic scholarships, it's kind of a tradition of air force brats to try that. I went to Annapolis for two years, and then I resigned. (personal interview, 2 August 1988)

Taylor's designs indicate a strong art influence mixed with a serious sense of discipline. Looking at his family background, one can clearly identify the influences. His art ability he credits to his mother:

I definitely came from an art background. When I was very young, I took private art lessons. My mother, who is a really good painter, was a major influence on me. That is where I got that ability to draw well. (personal interview, 2 August 1988)

He credits his father with establishing his sense of discipline:

> On the other hand, I played high school and college sports and was always very good in athletics, and that was my father's influence.

He recognizes both as major influences on his ability to be a good art director:

> So the discipline I learned, the self-discipline combined with the art background helps a lot in the organizational ability I have as a director. (personal interview, 2 August 1988)

In 1965 Taylor resigned from Annapolis and went to sea for a year as a ship's engineer. After returning, he entered the University of Utah's architecture program and then transferred to the art department, where he received his bachelor's degree in painting and sculpture.

After a series of moves from Utah to Berkeley, then back to Utah, he received a Cole Porter Fellowship to the University of Southern California (USC), where he earned a master's degree in printmaking and photography. His thesis was a videotape entitled *Star Car*.

> I projected the lightshow system in a television studio with the camera on it and made film chains and did real time video mixes through a Grass Valley switcher. That's what my thesis ended up being, a three-hour videotape, which was an MTV kind of metaphorical collage done to contemporary music. (personal interview, 2 August 1988)

In 1973, after completing his program at USC, Taylor decided it was time to choose a medium on which to concentrate and a direction to pursue:

> At some point you have to decide on some process that you are going to get involved with and you have to put energy into that process every day, and it will teach you. But you have to put energy into a process, and you can't do a little bit of everything. So, I decided on filmmaking, primarily a graphic approach to making film. (personal interview, 2 August 1988)

He approached Robert Abel with his portfolio, and was hired on the spot. This was just as Abel and Con Pederson were establishing their new studios. Taylor spent five years there. Taylor is responsible for

notably that first 7-Up commercial, bubbles where the girls come off of
the bottle and it turns into a whole lightshow. It was the history of 7-
Up, but it was supposed to look very much like a lightshow. (personal
interview, 2 August 1988)

These effects and the ABC *Sunday Night Movie* spots were effects
which Taylor was able to design with the help of his previous experience in light shows. After his graduation from Utah he designed a
lightshow called *Rainbow Jam* which toured the country.

I saw a Jerry Abram's headlight show. It was a lightshow from San Francisco. When I saw his show, I had an instantaneous flash as to how I
could do something similar to that. I could use projectors and project
different pieces of a picture that fit together like a painting by number
with light . . . Everything was planned out very methodically, all of the
imagery. We built these two big control panels that we ran it from. It was
very much like a musical instrument that you could play visually. That
was 'Rainbow Jam.' It became quite successful and toured with the Grateful Dead for a while and many other concerts. (personal interview, 2
August 1988)

Taylor worked for Abel for five years before they did *Star Trek, The
Motion Picture*. He was responsible for designing the miniatures and
storyboarding the effects sequences of the movie. He recalls:

I designed the *Enterprise* and the other models and supervised the building
of those. (personal interview, 2 August 1988)

Unfortunately, at that point, Abel had a conflict with Paramount and
they brought in Doug Trumbull to finish the production.

Taylor was asked by John Whitney, Jr. and Gary Demos to join
Triple I as creative director. He accepted and proceeded to

reorganize the place and redesign the interior and made it a working
studio, because they had been doing experiments of all different kinds
and they had done production for some things, but they were very disor-
ganized when it came to being a film production company. (personal
interview, 2 August 1988)

During that period he also produced the infamous computer-
generated character "Adam Powers." Taylor stayed with Triple I for
three years, which included the *TRON* project. Taylor supervised the
effects simulation for *TRON*, which involved coordinating the efforts

of Triple I, MAGI, Robert Abel and Associates, and Digital Effects. He explains:

> Part of what I do is very organizational in making a lot of these things work out. That's half the battle in a lot of design problems in motion pictures is to communicate to the number of people you have to and in a clear way. (personal interview, 2 August 1988)

After completing *TRON,* Taylor was asked by Philip Mittelman, MAGI president, to join MAGI as creative director and open a West Coast office. Taylor accepted. However, after establishing the MAGI West Coast operations he began to tire of computer simulation, and desired to return to more traditional filmmaking and direction. This resulted in a series of jobs working with Lucasfilm, Ladd Company, Lee-Lacey and Associates, and Apogee, where he still does the majority of his model work.

Taylor is presently with Image Point, which is the commercial division of Cannell films. He directs commercials.

> I'm directing commercials on a regular basis. I'm doing the 7-Up campaign with the little red dots that jump off the cans and get into trouble, and the Duracel and Kraft commercials. (personal interview, 2 August 1988)

Taylor no longer concentrates on one method, but like any well-versed artist or communicator, uses the tools which serve the message best.

> I try to make an objective decision about the combination of techniques to do a particular idea. I don't really favor any one particular technology. It's whatever works and whatever works economically. (Richard Taylor, personal interview, 2 August 1988)

7

Video Collaboration

Computer animation presents users with a variety of visual potential. It offers the ability not only to generate images, but also to create synthetic environments, manipulate realistic images, synthesize fabricated icons with natural images, and openly explore the physical, the psyche, and various discipline relationships. The use of video with the computer enhances this ability to generate and manipulate images and provides an even greater creative potential.

The collaboration between computers and video can be achieved by combining or synthesizing computer-generated imagery with either unaltered video images or manipulated video images. The computer can also be used to create a variety of effects, which are referred to as "computer processing" or "image processing." These uses defined the two camps which emerged within this new medium. One focused on synthesizing video and computer images and the other utilized the computer solely to create effects. Physicist and artist Lou Katz posits:

> The key with video was using computers to control the images and to create the effects as opposed to synthesizing the image. I still think that there is more soul and more life in a medium where the images are real. There's a different focus when you're out to synthesize an image that looks very real. (personal interview, 18 May 1988)

However, the opposing camp viewed synthesis as a new capability in order to explore and push the boundaries and confines of visual reality. Louise Etra Ledeen, aligned with this camp, argues:

> The reason why a lot of the people like ourselves made that transition was the equipment we had was very limited and we began to not only manipulate the visual reality, but also create a new reality to do synthesis. (Louise Etra-Ledeen, personal interview, 25 January 1988)

Video emerged as an art form in the 1960s after being introduced by Nam June Paik. Along with this evolving medium, three distinct schools of thought were established. Louise Etra Ledeen elaborates:

> There were three schools of video—the documentary group. There were the people who were involved in what is now called conceptual art, people like Bill Wegman, Peter Campus, and Vito Acconti. Then there were the people like ourselves who were involved in using video as an experimental medium. There were different names given to the school. It's called experimental video, abstract, where you're actually using the medium itself to distort images, or manipulate images and got involved in electronics. (personal interview, 25 January 1988)

The early video artists, like the pioneer computer animators, out of necessity developed their own tools. Some of the first were Bill Etra, who built the Rutt-Etra Synthesizer; Steven Beck, who designed the Direct Video Synthesizer; and Dan Sandin, who constructed the Sandin Image Processor.

Collaborators

Various collaborations materialized from the creation of these devices. Lou Katz who began working with Bill Etra in the mid-1970s, recalls:

> In the mid 1970s I met Bill Etra and we teamed up . . . we did some work together combining digital images and digital control of video special effects. We worked out a scheme for making animated color movies. Bill and I worked on some computer control of video special effects machines. We could modify images, we could combine images from a computer with live images. We made a tape in 1975, called "Ms. Muffett," which combined what is now called fractals with computer graphic drawings of some simple shapes, namely the spider web mixed with live images. (personal interview, 18 May 1988)

Dan Sandin, after arriving at the University of Illinois, embarked upon designing and building an analog image processor, which he completed in a year and a half.

> I decided to work on the analog image processor which was this idea of a visual analog of the MOOG synthesizer. I got a couple of small grants and it took about a year and a half. (personal interview, 9 February 1988)

Not long after he completed this project, Tom DeFanti, who designed the GRASS computer animation system while a graduate student at Ohio State University under Charles Csuri, arrived at the University of Illinois. He and Sandin joined forces. This cooperative effort initiated the amalgamation of resources and philosophies. Video and computer artist Jane Veeder elaborates:

> The Sandin Image Processor and GRASS, which was developed by Tom DeFanti, had to do with artists gaining access to what computers could do and in a way that gave them a lot of autonomy. Dan Sandin in particular was interested in developing self-teaching tools. That was the philosophy that pervaded the whole scene there. (personal interview, 26 January 1988)

DeFanti and Sandin's collaboration provided not only a different philosophical focus, but a new emphasis on standardizing equipment, encouraging compatibility. Lou Katz explains:

> In those days it made the most sense to have computers that could produce changing images, manipulate images, and where you could record them on videotape. Tom [DeFanti] and Dan [Sandin] realized that was the way to go. Nobody else went that way. There were incredibly awful computers where they chose to totally disregard the technical standards of video and they would make gorgeous pictures on the screen, but you couldn't record them. (Lou Katz, personal interview, 18 May 1988)

This is a medium which encourages collaboration, not only because of the dependence upon others to aid in the production of the art form, but in the sense of community which evolved along with the development of tools and philosophies. Louise Etra Ledeen asserts:

> A lot of people involved in computer graphics and video have a sense of community about them. Working in computer graphics and video is *not* a solitary art form, no matter how insular you want to be, you really need the help and assistance from other people. Either in terms of collaboration or environment (having access to facilities). Out of that necessity there have been a lot of 'odd couple' collaborations. There's a lot of sharing of information and technology. (personal interview, 25 January 1988)

I believe this sense of community and the emphasis on collaboration is the direct result of Sandin and DeFanti's consistent and compatible goals. Sandin defines them:

To summarize what distinguishes our approach from many approaches is that we're committed to, in general, have historically, and will continue to be, very low-cost to moderate-cost equipment . . . We've been committed to completely real time or very close to real time systems and interactive systems and low-cost systems. Another distinction is the way we relate to the art community. I had commitments to developing tools that artists could learn, not tools that did what artists already could do. You have to make it accessible and kind of conceptually clear and then artists can learn what they need to know, and they can use the tools. And we've been committed to developing and maintaining those tools for artists to use. (Dan Sandin, personal interview, 9 May 1988)

DAN SANDIN

As a child, Dan Sandin had aspirations of being a scientist. He realized this ambition with a master's degree and a Ph.D. in physics from the University of Wisconsin. However, after attaining candidacy he found he was becoming more interested in images and began diverting his attention in that direction.

While I was a researcher at the University of Wisconsin, I essentially started training myself in the area of using photography as a tool, doing a lot of optical processing, processing through bent pieces of Plexiglas and various projection techniques, optical and chemical, abstracted false color images. It occurred to me rather clearly that this could be done with electronics, the same kinds of processing. (Dan Sandin, personal interview, 9 February 1988)

However, his introduction to computers occurred during his undergraduate studies, where in 1963, he participated in a program sponsored by Argon Laboratories and learned how to program computers. Because of this early computer programming experience, Sandin was able to earn some of his assistantship money through computer programming.

His next exposure to computers also occurred at the University of Wisconsin:

Also at University of Wisconsin I was exposed to 'The Classic Link,' which was a laboratory instrument computer which is a predecessor of the modern personal computer, without question, in that it had interactive text editors, it was a very real time system. The computer was essentially designed to monitor laboratory experiments, so by its nature was an interactive computer. It read dials and did graphics. (personal interview, 9 February 1988)

The third computer Sandin encountered was while in graduate school:

> While I was doing research at the physics lab, there was a highly inter-active computer system there that ran the particle accelerator. The computer was so advanced that it ran the particle accelerator in fore-ground, which meant that you could do anything you wanted in the background, while that was happening. It was in a sense like a multitask machine. It had a graphic output display, so I was making pictures. I was able to do graphics on this machine. (Dan Sandin, personal interview, 9 February 1988)

This equipment was very close to the equipment that Ken Knowlton used at Bell Laboratories, although this was a black-and-white system and Knowlton's had color displays:

> The DDP 124 was the machine we used, the machine he [Knowlton] used was the DDP 224. (Dan Sandin, personal interview, 9 February 1988)

In 1971, after completing his work at the University of Wisconsin, Sandin was offered a position with the University of Illinois, Chicago Campus, then called Chicago Circle. His exhibition record, in con-junction with his scientific background made him a likely prospect for the art department at Chicago Circle, for they were considered a third-generation Bauhaus institution that focused on the marriage of technology and fine arts. Sandin explains:

> They [Chicago Circle] were a kind of third-generation Bauhaus, so their idea was the obvious thing to do at this time. The new school was to combine industrial technology, the fine art tradition, with what was called at that time Cybernetic age. They hired me because they thought I could make a contribution. That was 1971. (personal interview, 9 February 1988)

After getting settled in at Chicago Circle, Sandin decided to pursue building the visual version of the MOOG synthesizer, the Sandin analog image processor. Soon after he completed the project, he was contacted by Phil Morton,

> who was head of video at the Art Institute of Chicago. He said he wanted very much to copy it [the Sandin image processor]. We worked together for a year and created documentation on the image processor. It was one year of Fridays. We created this documentation that was actually good

enough for an extremely dedicated individual, with about $3,000, to build a very powerful image processing environment. (Dan Sandin, personal interview, 9 February 1988)

Just as this project was coming to an end, Tom DeFanti arrived, and Sandin and DeFanti—who had met previously—began combining their devices and working together. In 1973 they set up the "Circle Graphics Habitat," which was established to provide an educational media environment. The facility served as the creative center for educational materials and several video works.

The next project which the Sandin-DeFanti team tackled was the Z box system.

We started the Z box system in the late 1970s. Tom did all the software development for the system. I did a little bit of the hardware development for it. And mainly some of the accessories, like the TV going in and some of the details to make the TV come out right. (Dan Sandin, personal interview, 9 February 1988)

Sandin's next project was an unsuccessful solo journey in which he attempted to design a digital image processor. He had been awarded an NEA grant and a Rockefeller grant.

After the analog image processor success, I set upon the task of designing a digital image processor, essentially computer-based. I worked on it for years and was not successful in completing that project. I had good support if I had chosen something on the appropriate scale. It was a classic error of taking too big a bite. (Dan Sandin, personal interview, 9 February 1988)

Sandin's more recent work has been in computer holography, three-dimensional image processing, and scolograms. He is also working with mathematician Lou Kauffman on the visualization of mathematical objects.

The work I'm doing now has been in collaboration of course with Tom's system, and working on this three-dimensional image processor. I was doing computer-generated holography. I did that for about two years. (Dan Sandin, personal interview, 9 February 1988)

JANE VEEDER

Raised in Los Angeles, Jane Veeder comes from a strong but varied fine arts background—four years in a professional repertory theatre,

Frame from *A Volume of Two-Dimensional Julia Sets.* **Dr. Daniel J. Sandin.**

ten years in ceramic sculpture, photography, and installation, prior to video. She entered the ceramic sculpture graduate program at the Chicago Art Institute, but after Phil Morton introduced her to video, she changed her emphasis. Through Morton, she met the computer electronic arts community—Dan Sandin and Tom DeFanti—and became quickly acquainted with analog computers. In describing that coalition she states:

> Everybody in that scene learned to do everything, collaborated on everything, from language development to hardware design to artmaking. (personal interview, 26 January 1988)

The ZGRASS machine, which emerged in 1981, was Veeder's first instrument in computer graphics.

> This machine's capabilities were real time animation and real time sound synthesis (its videogame heritage) accessed by a custom language optimized for interactive artmaking, all wrapped up together like a hot little sports car. Also, it was the only affordable computer graphics system on the planet at that time that output NTSC composite video! We were doing interactive installations, animations, sending out tapes everywhere!

It was an extraordinarily productive and, for me, evolutionary period. (Jane Veeder, personal interview, 26 January 1988)

Interactive installations like Veeder's *Warpitout* began to surface, and artists began to record animations on tape. ZGRASS succeeded in offering a capable and affordable tool to the arts community.

Veeder's first completely computer-animated piece was *Montana,* completed in 1982. It was generated with footage from Veeder's summer camping travels with Morton.

Every year my partner and I would drive out into the Mountain West, camping and doing video/audio. I travelled with relief maps, geological highway maps, bird books, and so on. I loved the physical world out there and its attendant information space. As I got more into graphics programming, I wanted to pull the elements of that travel and video work into the digital domain. I used computer graphics to get at the views and processes not accessible to my video camera, but moreover as a synthetic medium in which to interact with ALL the elements . . . images, geo processes, info associations, and future fantasies. (Jane Veeder, personal interview, 26 January 1988)

The same year Veeder made *Montana,* she created *Warpitout,* which offers real time color graphics processing of the viewer's or participant's face. Veeder states it was based on

an existing application of analog technology. The "IP [Image Processor] Photo Booth" was a standard video art event in Chicago. The player could manipulate simple controls to colorize and otherwise process a video image of their face, then signal the IPist to snap a polaroid. With *Warpitout,* I translated that into a digital game where people could learn a bit of elementary computer graphics, e.g. fills, menus, simple geometry, drawing with bitmaps, and experience how marvelous the Zgrass machine's videogame hardware really was (apart from killing aliens). In both situations the lure was being able to maniplute one's own image. (personal interview, 26 January 1988)

Veeder's next two works were related. The first was *Floater,* a six-minute piece which she describes as representing

the total integration and manifestation of everything I knew at that point. (personal interview, 26 January 1988)

Her next piece was *Visgame,* which was exhibited at the San Francisco SIGGRAPH Art Show. It consisted of the last sequence of *Floater* which was placed in an interactive mode.

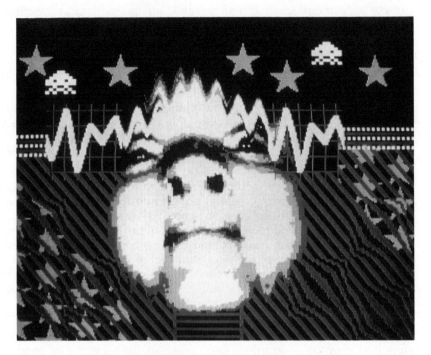

From *Warpitout*. Jane Veeder.

At that time my philosophy was that computer art had to be interactive. (personal interview, 26 January 1988)

In 1985 Veeder was commissioned by the Pacific Northwest College of Art in Portland, Oregon to set up a computer graphics laboratory. After completing that project she joined Wavefront Technology in Santa Barbara, California in 1986, where she was a prototype interface designer. She is currently teaching in San Francisco at California State University.

FRANK DIETRICH

Frank Dietrich's background is in media studies. In the early 1970s he attended the newly established Institute for the Science of Media, which was part of the Technical University in Berlin. He studied the theoretical, the historical, and the practical video work. While there, he, along with two friends, founded "Telepublic Berlin," whose function was utilizing video as a medium that could enable people to talk back to big network channels. (Frank Dietrich, personal interview, 21 January 1988)

In 1975 Dietrich received a grant from the German Academic Exchange Service to study computer graphics in the United States. He chose the Chicago Circle after visiting a number of places in the United States. He explains his reasons for this choice:

It seemed to me one of the few places at the time that was particularly interested in three things that I thought was pretty interesting. One is to combine the world of video with the world of computer graphics. . . . Secondly, the whole notion of interactivity. My understanding of animation is something that is not just like film, the sequencing of single still frames, but rather is the representation of simulation of certain aspects of life. Third, what is today being understood as user interfaces, at large, mainly the issue of making this technology comprehensible and usable by people whose profession and whose lives have nothing to do with machines. (personal interview, 21 January 1988)

Dietrich's arrival coincided with the height of the ZGRASS movement. He stayed in Chicago from 1979 through 1981 and completed a master's degree in Electronic Visualization at the University of Illinois. He then moved to Los Angeles and taught at West Coast College for one year, followed by a move to the Silicon Valley in northern California. Presently Dietrich is with Silicon Graphics in Cologne, Germany.

Dietrich has been collaborating with his wife, Zsuzsa Molnar, in video, computer graphics, and performance art for several years, beginning in Chicago with ZGRASS. One of their collaborations was *Sanke,* generated on ZGRASS in 1982. However, Dietrich abandoned ZGRASS in 1983 (Jankel and Morton 1984, 84).

LARRY CUBA

Larry Cuba studied architecture at Washington University in St. Louis, where he learned computer programming. After graduating in 1972, his growing interest in filmmaking and computer graphics prompted his move to Los Angeles to attend CalArts graduate school in filmmaking and animation. He was also hoping to work with John Whitney, Sr. He explains:

At that time there were only three or four artists doing computer animation. There was John Whitney, who had done work at IBM center, then there was Lillian Schwartz and Stan VanderBeek who had worked with Ken Knowlton at Bell Labs. That's really why I went to Los Angeles. I ultimately wanted to work with him [John Whitney Sr.] and find out how you did computer animation. (Larry Cuba, personal interview, 18 January 1988)

Whitney was open to the possibility of Cuba working as his apprentice; however, at that time, he did not have a computer, nor access to a facility. That soon changed, for arrangements were made for his use of Triple I's computer system. He contacted Cuba to program for him in exchange for the use of Triple I's facilities and use of his optical printer. They worked for a year on what was to become Whitney's film, *Arabesque*. Cuba recalls:

We worked at Triple I on *Arabesque*. For a year working only on weekends. Then he [Whitney] worked on the material we generated at Triple I on his printer for another six months to a year, just re-photographing and colorizing material. (personal interview, 18 January 1988)

After completing Whitney's film, Cuba began working on his own film, *Two Space*. By 1977 he had generated much material which eventually became *Two Space*. He explains:

In 1979 I made *Two Space* out of material I had programmed and filmed in 1977. I made another film in 1978 called "378," but I think of *Two Space* as the earlier film because of the order in which the ideas evolved. (personal interview, 18 January 1988)

Cuba made his first computer film *First Fig,* in 1974, while a student at CalArts, Valencia.

In 1974, I made my first film. Personal computers didn't come along until years later. The only computers that existed at that time were mainframes owned by large institutions. Getting free access to these computers for an art proejct involved a lot of negotiating and red tape. My access, when granted, was limited to after work hours, so I ended up producing these films by working at night and sleeping during the day. (personal interview, 18 January 1988)

In 1975, Cuba left California and went to Chicago where he worked on Tom DeFanti's GRASS system. He describes it:

Everything was controlled with dials. The idea was to emulate a musical instrument that was performed live. The system was fast enough to pro-

Still from the film *3/78*. Larry Cuba.

duce animation in real time which allowed for live performance. (personal interview, 19 January 1988)

However, it soon became apparent that GRASS did not suit Cuba's purposes, for it was too oriented to real time play versus programmability (Cuba, written correspondence, January 22, 1991):

> Because my work is experimental, it is very important that I generate images quickly so I can try things out, see the results immediately, then perform the next experiment based on those results. Having a fast turnaround time is more important to me than photorealistic rendering which is currently too time consuming for experimental work.

> I've also concentrated on the choreography of the forms in my films. I'm interested in visual perception and by using black and white imagery, I've been able to create subtle perceptual effects that aren't possible using color. My focus has always been on movement and rhythm. (personal interview, 18 January 1988)

So he dismissed the GRASS system for his personal work and returned to Los Angeles to do programming for Robert Abel and Associates. A few months later he was asked to submit a bid for a computer animation sequence for *Star Wars*. He was awarded the contract and returned to Chicago in 1976 to work with the GRASS system. After three months of work, the result was

> the simulation of a computer diagram of the 'Death Star' which the rebel pilots watch during their briefing session. (Perlman 1980, 2)

After *Star Wars*, he returned to LA and began work on "Two Space" at Triple I. During this time, work continued on the GRASS language in Chicago. The developer of the language, Tom DeFanti, added features that gave the programmer precise control over the timing of graphic events, an improvement that enticed Cuba to return to Chicago and use the GRASS system to produce his film, "3/78."

> Since there was only one machine that ran the GRASS language, access was limited, but Professor DeFanti was anxious for more artists to use his language. At that time, the components being used in microcomputers were just beginning to become powerful enough for graphics, so a personal system was developed that was affordable for the individual. The processor in the new machine was called the Z-50, so when the GRASS language was rewritten, the new version was called ZGRASS. (personal interview, 18 January 1988)

In 1981 Cuba received a grant from the American Film Institute (AFI) to make a film. Tired of having to seek access to institutional facilities, he admits spending the money on a ZGRASS machine.

> Now I had my own system. Although it was very small, I could have it in my own studio and work at my own schedule. (personal interview, January 18, 1988)

He used ZGRASS langauge to produce *Calculated Movements* which he completed in 1985. It premiered at the San Francisco Museum of Modern Art.

That was the last film Cuba finished. However, in 1988 he received a grant from the National Endowment for the Arts to produce another film. Cuba asserts that the focus of his work is movement:

> Because my work is experimental it is very important that I generate a lot of imagery quickly, that I can try things and see the results and try the next thing based on the results. That turn around time is more important than having it look like glass or chrome or some other kind of lighting effect because I've concentrated on choreography of these objects.

You notice they're all in black and white, even the color is not important to me. It's all focused on movement and rhythm. (personal interview, 28 January 1988)

ED EMSHWILLER

Ed Emshwiller was born in Lansing, Michigan in 1925. He received his B.A. in 1949 in art from the University of Michigan and proceeded to study painting at the Ecole des Beaux Arts in Paris. He made his first film in 1959, *Dance Chromatic,* which incorporated animation with live action and received an Award of Exceptional Merit from the Creative Film Foundation. His next two films also used animation: *Transformations,* which he completed in 1959 and *Life Lines* made in 1960.

In the early sixties Emshwiller worked as a cameraman for television documentaries and independent film productions. During this period he was exposed to his first computer animation. He recalled, in an 1988 interview:

In the early 60s I was a cameraman on a Canadian television documentary on computers called 'The Quiet Takeover.' I saw at MIT early vector computer graphics that impressed me. They had a space program where things were flying around . . . They were also doing various explorations of image recognition. Things like when does Z turn into N. And they were doing music. The computer was playing Bach, as I recall. I was impressed by all those things. Those were the first live on-site computer animation that I encountered. (personal interview, 14 January 1988)

In 1966 Emshwiller received a Ford Foundation grant which he used to create his film *Relativity.* In 1970, he began to concentrate on video:

My reason for going to video, basically, was to explore the possibilities of keying, mixing, and transforming images. (Russett and Starr 1976, 207)

His first piece during this period was an autobiographical work entitled *Images Of Ed Emshwiller.* His second was *Computer Graphics #1,* which he produced through the WNET Television Lab, where he was introduced to the scanimate synthesizer. His piece *Thermogenesis* was a variation on *Computer Graphics #1.* The third videotape was *Scape-mates,* which he completed in 1972. Russett and Starr assert that:

Still from *Sunstone*. Ed Emshwiller.

By using this scanimate synthesizer, he has been able to explore the emotional effects of simultaneous imagery, the interplay of abstract animated environments, and the dramatization of surrealistic events. (1976, 206)

In 1979 Emshwiller was invited to NYIT by Alvy Ray Smith and Ed Catmull. His prior experience in animation at that point had been with the scanimate, which was an analog computer system which operated in real time, very different to NYIT's facilities. He revealed:

When I went to NYIT and Ed and Alvy asked me what I wanted to do, I went there with experience in analog computer graphics, which is real time image manipulation. I thought I could do a great deal in a fairly short time. Prior to that I had been fascinated by computer graphics I had seen, and wrote a script for an hour-and-a-half television program. I told them I wanted to do an hour-and-a-half program and they thought that was very funny. They knew it would take a very long time. (personal interview, 14 January 1988)

During the eight months he was there, he produced a three-minute animation, *Sunstone,* which he described as dealing with

energy as the fundamental source of all being, in its various manifestation as pure energy or light, as inorganic rock, stone, sand, as organic wood, flesh, as living beings, faces, eyes, as the imagination of mankind, art, fantasy, stone truth. So it's an exploration, a tapestry, a collage of reflections on the journey through various ways in which to see energy, energy as a reflection of all its various forms. (personal interview, 14 January 1988)

During *Sunstone* Enshwiller worked with Alvy Ray Smith. Smith's recollections of the collaborative effort and of the artist he worked with were:

This guy [Emshwiller] has true artistic sensitivity, but he also loves technology, enough to put up with the hard edges of the early technology. To me he's a real artist. He doesn't just make pictures, he explores the edges of the culture.

I think the partnership worked so well on "Sunstone" because he was the principal artist, no question about it. We did it together in a sense. He needed the technological help, which I provided, but I'm an artist, that's where I came from. This was my chance to learn from a master. So I got to reach toward the art part with my best technology and he got to reach toward the technology part with his best art. It worked great! (personal interview, 19 May 1988)

Emshwiller displayed no preference towards any particular medium. He maintained:

A lot has to do with access, a lot has to do with particular ideas I'm fascinated with at the time. I am fascinated by the interaction of tools and imagination, and I find exploring possibilities of my imagination interacting with these tools very satisfying. (personal interview, 14 January 1988)

One of Ed Emshwiller's hot works was a collaborative piece which employed several media, including an Amiga computer.

I'm completing a piece which combines, and this is something that I do a great deal of, I've never been a purist in the art forms. I use whatever seems to make that part of the image most effective and what I can do most efficiently. Using video where video makes sense and computers where it makes sense, then I usually combine them. My current project which I am completing was first a multimedia stage production where we used computers in a different way. I had a special switcher made, used by Amiga to control the display of sixteen different video display systems, monitors, and screens on stage, and select eight different sources, cameras, special effects generators, video tapes. And these could be under computer control and distributed to these different display surfaces at a very rapid rate or at any rate you wanted. (personal interview, 14 January 1988)

The computer's role in this production is different than that of graphics generator, but it indeed is involved in image creation.

Here's a case of using computers as an artistic assisting device, but it wasn't specifically making computer graphics, it was making a stage presentation of video which included computer graphics and within that there are images that involve video and computer graphics. (Ed Emshwiller, personal interview, 14 January 1988)

In July 1990, the art field suffered the loss of not only a great artist, but a wonderfully warm and creative man, Ed Emshwiller.

VIBEKE SORENSEN

Vibeke Sorensen originally came from Copenhagen, Denmark. In 1957 she came to the United States with her family. They initially settled in Chicago, but upon her eighth birthday they moved to Buffalo, New York. When she was sixteen she returned to Denmark to study architecture. Upon graduation she returned to the United States for graduate school.

I have a background in architecture and I really wanted to realize my creations. At that time, in Denmark especially, 80 percent of architects were unemployed and very few practicing architects were under forty-five. I was twenty. (personal interview, 14 January 1988)

The realization that she would most likely be building models for other architects was not very appealing. So she began to consider other alternatives.

I had been following film and video and I thought film was similar to architecture in that you're dealing with physical aspects of your medium, and you're also dealing with aesthetics. (personal interview, 14 January 1988)

In 1974 she became interested in computers and was one of the first artists to have access to the very first digital video effects device.

In 1974, the Electronic Music Studio in London introduced the first digital video effects device, engineered by artist Richard Monkhouse, as a system specifically for musicians and artists. Vibeke Sorensen and Tom DeWitt were among the first to experiment on it. (Goodman 1987, 171)

Although excited about this new equipment development, Sorensen also realized that there was a sacrifice involved. In order to obtain the precision this device offered, movement was abandoned. This was a difficult adjustment since she had been working in animation prior to this development.

> I discovered video synthesis and that was really great because it involved physics and the aesthetic. But the problem was precise control. And so I gave up movement for precision, when I first started working with digital graphics. (personal interview, 14 January 1988)

However, the current technology supports her interests in movement and environment, which stem from her foundation in architecture.

> I think the most interesting work is interactive or environmental responsive. I'm also interested in 3-D and it's amazing how fast that's coming back with the technology, because it's so easy to make a three-dimensional environment with the computer and then to simulate movement through it. (personal interview, 14 January 1988)

With great relief she exclaims:

> Finally we have a medium in which we can create those kind of experiences that work and we can make them move! (personal interview, 14 January 1988)

Sorensen is presently on the faculty at CalArts Valencia, teaching computer graphics and computer animation. Her current artwork focuses on stereoscopic imaging and three-dimensional graphics.

> I've been doing a lot of work with stereoscopic imaging. Because the potential to perceive the space is there. I've been really interested in video that utilizes that capability to create imaginary environments. I'm doing very formal abstract kind of motion graphics related to music, and I'm also doing computer images which are stereoscopic.

> I try to do work that not only references the technology I'm working with, but is also a kind of visual one liner. (personal interview, 14 January 1988)

Left eye views.

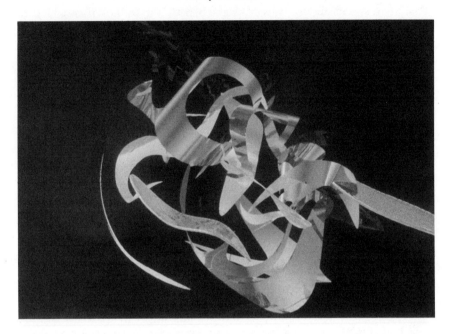

Two sets of stereoscopic freeze frames from *Maya*. For cross-eyed viewing.
Vibeke Sorensen.

Right eye views.

8

Contemporary View

The contemporaries can be divided into three groups: computer animation production houses, institutions, and individuals. The animation houses which have emerged during this period have been Metrolight, Rhythm and Hues, and Kroyer Films. These companies materialized after the great falls of Robert Abel and Associates, Digital Productions, Omnibus, and Cranston-Csuri. Consequently, they also capitalized on the talent that was then available, such as Con Pederson from Robert Abel and Associates, who is now with Metrolight. John Hughes, Charlie Gibson, and others from Abel established Rhythm and Hues.

The surviving computer houses such as Pacific Data Inc. (PDI) and Pixar, also have inherited talent such as Michael Collery, formerly with Cranston-Csuri, and John Lasseter, who left Disney to join Pixar in 1984. These companies continue to produce quality work such as Pixar's 1989 Academy Award winner *Tin Toy* and PDI's 1988 SIGGRAPH Film Video Show exhibit *Burning Love*.

Some of the institutions which pioneered computer animation have withdrawn from the arena, including the Jet Propulsion Laboratory (JPL) and The National Research Council of Canada (NRCC). Marceli Wein from the NRCC explains:

> We essentially decided that as a national laboratory with the industrial objectives and goals, we found that it was inappropriate for us to continue. It was becoming more commercial, and one had to produce. It was time for us to get back to more engineering and design research and let the artistic work continue elsewhere. (personal interview, 3 August 1988)

Some founding institutions not only continue computer animation research and production, but have expanded their philosophies and facilities. These organizations include California Institute of Technology, MIT, University of Illinois at Chicago, and Ohio State University (OSU). Chuck Csuri formerly of Ohio State University described the developments occurring at Ohio State University in 1988:

> I have a major supercomputer graphics project that involves four-and-a-half million dollars over five years, and by next summer I'll have ten full-time people working on that kind of development, so that software runs on the Cray, Sun Microcomputer, IBM PC, MacIntosh. I think this could go a long way towards making software available to many arts programs, because it's going to be licensed at far less cost than commercial software. Then, in addition to that, my center is being funded. By next summer I'll have eighteen full-time people and eight doctoral students working on mainly software. For the first time we'll have major resources. We'll have about six million dollars to work with to do this development. (personal interview, 18 November 1987)

Many of the pioneering individuals have left the field, such as Ken Knowlton, who is presently with Wang Laboratories conducting research on "the paperless office" and A. Michael Noll, who is currently at University of Southern California, focusing on "the illiteracy towards technology which exists" (personal interview, 9 May 1988), and Charles Csuri who retired from Ohio State University.

However, most have remained, including John Whitney, Sr., and James Blinn. Others have remained linked to the field, but in different areas; for example Robert Abel, who is presently consulting with Apple computer:

> I'm working in other areas related to computers. I'm particularly fascinated by the development of CDI and CD ROM, and I'm consulting with Apple. (personal interview, 9 May 1988)

Most of the artists, including Larry Cuba, John Whitney, Sr., and David Em, are continuing their pursuit of their personal expression through computer animation. However, some, like Vibeke Sorenson and Dan Sandin, have begun to mix computer animation with other media.

There are two further individuals who appeared during this contemporary period, Heinz Otto-Peitgen and John Lasseter. Both employ computer animation in very different ways, Peitgen in the visualization of mathematical concepts, and Lasseter in the creation of character animation. Both were trained in the disciplines in which they use computer animation, rather than in computer science (Peitgen in mathematics and Lasseter in traditional Disney character animation). Both represent current directions in which computer animation is proceeding.

HEINZ OTTO-PEITGEN

Heinz Otto-Peitgen grew up in Germany and attended the University of Bonn to pursue studies in mathematics and physics. He was introduced to computers in 1968, and was torn between a fascination with computers and a strong interest in pure mathematics. However, one of his professors at the University of Bonn resolved that dilemma by suggesting

> that I should do a thesis using the computer to do some very deep calculations in mathematics, and that had never been done before on the computer. (personal interview, 3 August 1988)

He completed that research and returned to pure mathematics. After a few years concentrating on abstract mathematics, he began to consider

> that there should be more than the static joy of doing mathematics and this abstract world, that there should be a link with the real world, so I began looking for applications. (personal interview, 3 August 1988)

In the late 1970s, while at the University of Bremen, Peitgen became interested in the Chaos theory and began to consider conducting experiments with computers:

> I had this idea to try to do experiments on computers, in particular, use computer graphic devices to generate pictures of the experiments. Typically, the experiments which I did were of a kind that I would not get out just a few numbers, but one would get out tons of numbers. The only way it seemed to analyze for us, to generate pictures out of those numbers and then use the visual capability to somehow look closely, then properly, was into complex phenomena. (personal interview, 3 August 1988)

Peitgen and his colleagues began using the computer to construct drawings of mathematical computations which would illustrate the stages of a phenomenon in time he was investigating. Individual static graphics were soon linked together to produce animations, a series of images which illustrated the development of this phenomenon in time. Peitgen explains:

The point of our studies was that we had these ideas about objects, but we had no idea whatsoever how those would look if we would turn them into pictures. That was very exciting. And the most exciting part came when we started to animate those pictures, introduce the time evolution of them. That was 1981. (personal interview, 3 August 1988)

In 1982 Peitgen went on sabbatical to the University of Utah. He approached the chairman of the department of computer science, Richard Riesenfeld, with a proposition to work on a project which focused on the visualization of mathematical problems. Riesenfeld refused at first, however, he eventually agreed to allow Peitgen and two of his students access to University of Utah's computer facilities. Peitgen describes the work produced during that four-month period:

We produced numerous images which then became very well-known as fractals, and we did our first real animations. This was 1982. The animations we did at this time were animations which showed how fractal structures change. (personal interview, 3 August 1988)

He returned to Germany in the spring of 1983 and began to raise funds for equipment. By the end of 1983 he had set up his own laboratory and begun producing mathematical fractal images.

In 1984, the German Institute for Scientific Movies approached Peitgen and his research group with a proposition to produce a film focusing on one of the Chaos paradigms, the Lorenz Attractor.

The Lorenz Attractor is a discovery which was made using the computer, by this great man, Ed Lorenz, at MIT in Cambridge Massachusetts, in the 1960s. In the 1970s it was understood that it was a breakthrough discovery in understanding phenomena like turbulence, phenomena like the unpredictability in weather formation, and the development of climate.

It is a genuine mathematical object which you can visualize, and as you do that you can see a sort of geometric figure which essentially has two leaves or two ears or sheets and they're strangely connected to each other. The point is that there are certain dynamics occurring on these two sheets of that geometrical object. But the motion is very complicated and complex. So we did this animation explaining how this motion takes place. (Heinz Otto Peitgen, personal interview, 3 August 1988)

This film, *Fly Lorenz,* also illustrated how this object evolves.

Heinz Otto Peitgen has been a faculty member in mathematics at University of Bremen since 1977. In 1985 he was offered a position with the mathematics department at the University of California at Santa Cruz. Presently he maintains both positions and continues his work in the visualization of mathematical concepts. His current work focuses on another fractal, the "Mandelbrot Set," the most complex fractal known:

> My current work is still in fractals and we are just in the middle of doing a very painful animation. We want to create a movie on the "Mandelbrot Set." (Heinz Otto-Peitgen, personal interview, 3 August 1988)

JOHN LASSETER

John Lasseter grew up in Whittier, California. He is a product of the character animation program at the California Institute of the Arts, known as CalArts Valencia, which was founded by Walt Disney. Lasseter, when describing the program, reveals the Disney-influenced training he received:

> It was a program that was taught by old Disney animators and artists, teaching the Disney style of character animation. (personal interview, 19 May 1988)

During Lasseter's four years (1975–1979) at CalArts he produced two films, *Nitemare* and *Lady and the Lamp,* both of which won student academy awards for animation. These were preludes to his 1989 Academy Award for best animated short film (for *Tin Toy)*.

Immediately after completing his program at CalArts in 1979, Lasseter was hired by Disney Studios as an animator, and he worked in the story department for five years. During that period he worked with MAGI.

> We did a computer graphics test combining hand drawn character animation with computer generated backgrounds. It was called the 'Wild Things Test.' I designed and directed that and created it along with Glen Keane, another animator at Disney. That was my first venture into computer graphics. We were trying to get it to blend with Disney style animation. (John Lasseter, personal interview, 19 May 1988)

This experience opened up a new avenue for Lasseter. He began to learn about the computer animation industry and met some of the leading individuals involved in the industry. While visiting Lucasfilm, he met Alvy Ray Smith and Ed Catmull, who hired him on the spot at a conference in 1984. He recalls:

Still from *Luxo Jr.* John Lasseter. Copyright 1986 Pixar.

Ed Catmull asked me, while we were at a small conference at the Queen Mary, if I'd be interested in coming up and working with them on doing character animation with a computer. (personal interview, 19 May 1988)

Lasseter's first film at Lucasfilm was *The Adventures of Andre and Wally B*. Lasseter created all the movement in the film with a key frame animation system. *Luxo Jr.* was his next film venture in 1986, after the break with Lucasfilm and under the newly established Pixar. It won a series of international film and animation awards including the prestigious "Silver Bear" at the Berlin Film Festival. In 1987, he worked on *Red's Dream*. This was quite a challenge, for this film consisted of two segments—a reality section and a fantasy phase. Lasseter's most recent film, completed in 1988, was multi-award-winner *Tin Toy*.

Current Directions

Currently, two of the leading directions in which computer animation appears to be moving include scientific visualization, and medical applications. Kellogg Booth, chair of SIGGRAPH posits:

Medical imaging has been one of the big applications of computer graphics, one of the big things driving government funding and development. They're big consumers of the latest and greatest technology. (personal interview, 1 August 1988)

Examples of medical imaging applications include aiding the planning of surgery procedures, and therapy and treatment design.

Mathematician Heinz Otto Peitgen asserts:

animation for reason of scientific visualization is just at its beginning and really has a future, and will have an impact on the future in many ways. (personal interview, 3 Augusut 1988)

Scientific visualization covers applications from Nelson Max's molecule modeling and Thomas Banchoff's mathematical conceptualization to work produced utilizing SciAn, the visualization package developed by the Scientific Visualization Group at the Super Computations Research Institute (SCRI) on the Florida State University, Tallahassee campus. SciAn was designed specifically to aid scientists with their visualization efforts.

SCRI is an illustration of the current movement towards interdisciplinary and multi-disciplinary collaborations. Established in 1984, SCRI was the first university-based industrial governmental partnership to focus on research and training specifically in computational science and technology. A cooperative venture between Florida State University, the U.S. Department of Energy's Office of Energy Research, Control Data Corporation, ETA Systems Inc. and the State of Florida, SCRI gathers a team of scientists, engineers and technicians from a range of disciplines to problem solve.

SCRI is indeed a realization of the current trend of scientific visualization as described by Eric Pepke, head of SCRI's visualization group:

Another problem that we want to solve with SciAn is to bring video animation to the level where it can actually be used in the process of research.

If you want to use an animation as an educational tool maybe it's all right to take six weeks to design and layout and put together, or six months, but if you want to see how your model is performing today you don't have that amount of time. So I built into SciAn a way of making movies that only takes a couple hours or overnight to make a simple animation.

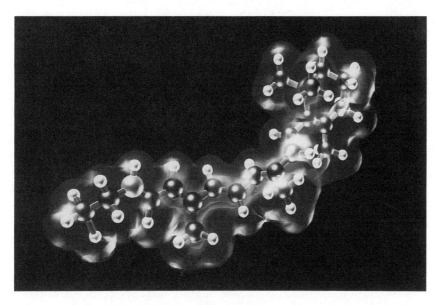

Electronic Field Density Visualization. SCRI/The Florida State University.

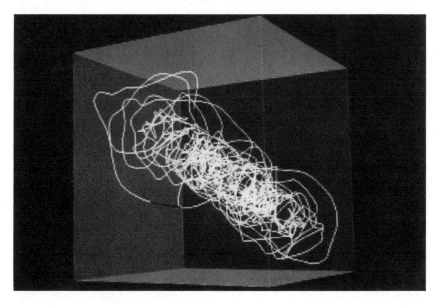

Electroencephalagram Data Simulation (one electrode). SCRI/The Florida State University.

And that has proved very useful, for if you can use an animation in the early stages of research and the development model, you can use it as a debugging tool, to see what's wrong with your model. (Eric Pepke, personal interview, 4 March, 1992)

The quest for increased realism and natural images continues. Phillip Mittelman, former president of MAGI, asserts:

There's been a real pronounced trend for the last few years to make it [computer animation] as realistic as possible, so that we could compete with and find the market in films and areas where you have to build models and do special effects, you could do them by computer. So there's a big thrust to be able to be as natural as possible. (personal interview, 11 May 1988)

Alvy Ray Smith's concurrence with Mittelman was obvious when he outlined Pixar's current goals:

Increased complexity of reality, richer and richer scenes, they're going to get longer too. We're up to four minutes now. (personal interview, 19 May 1988)

Character animation is an area which appears to be emerging as a focal point in computer animation design and development. Pixar lead this trend with *Luxo Jr.* in 1986 and *Tin Toy* in 1988. However, the current trend is moving toward a melding of forms: a blending of computer animation with live action animation and a seamless combination of computer animation with traditional animation.

9

Conclusions

There were seven major centers of activity in the formative years of computer animation: Salt Lake City, Utah; Columbus, Ohio; Los Angeles and the San Francisco Bay Areas in California; Old Westbury, New York; Murray Hill, New Jersey; and Cambridge, Massachusetts. Each represented a focal point where institutional and individual work was taking place. The University of Utah, David Evans, and Ivan Sutherland established Salt Lake City as a center. Ohio State University, Chuck Csuri, and later Cranston-Csuri asserted Columbus, Ohio as a founding city of computer animation. The Los Angeles area had several contributors: CalTech, JPL, and the film and television industry, in conjunction with John Whitney, Sr., James Blinn, David Em, Larry Cuba, and Robert Abel. The San Francisco Bay area also had several contributing institutions and individuals: Stanford, the University of Calilfornia at Berkeley, Lawrence Livermore Laboratories, Xerox PARC, and later PDI and Lucasfilm; the individuals include George Michael, Richard Shoup, Alvy Ray Smith, Nelson Max, and later Ed Catmull, Loren Carpenter, and Carl Rosendahl. New York Institute of Technology established Old Westbury, New York as a center, where Alvy Ray Smith and Ed Catmull worked, along with various artists such as Ed Emshwiller and Vibeke Sorensen, who both served as artists-in-residence there. Bell Laboratories, Ken Knowlton, A. Michael Noll, Stan VanderBeek, and Lillian Schwartz all insured Murray Hill as one of the founding major centers of computer animation. Cambridge, the home of MIT, the Whirlwind computer, and Ivan Sutherland's graduating institution, dictated its rightful place as an early center. Although many changes have taken place in the industry, some commercial institutions have folded, and individuals have since retired or changed research focus or art medium, these locations remain the major centers in the industry.

These centers have created support for the cooperative relationship between artists and scientists in this medium, for they serve equally as art centers. Artists Roy Lichtenstein, George Siegal, and Chuck Csuri were products of Ohio State University's art program. Both Los Angeles and the Bay Area are considered art centers of the world. MIT's Media Laboratory and NYIT's Graphics Laboratory have established both Cambridge and Old Westbury as supportive art communities. A strong arts patronage, in conjunction with supportive technology, advocates and promotes a secure environment for the collaboration between the arts and technology and artists and scientists.

Many of these institutions have encouraged an alliance between science and the arts. Chuck Csuri's art background was a major influence in the programs developed and the work produced at Ohio State University and Cranston-Csuri. CalTech and JPL both offered access to their facilities to artists such as David Em, John Whitney, Sr., Larry Cuba, and Vibeke Sorensen. New York Institute of Technology and Bell Laboratories created working environments which encouraged and supported joint ventures between artists and scientists. The results of their efforts were the collaborations between Ken Knowlton and Stan VanderBeek, and Ken Knowlton and Lillian Schwartz at Bell Labs and Ed Emshwiller and Alvy Ray Smith and David DeFrancisco at NYIT. However, one important factor in both of these situations was the availability of consistent financial support.

Many of the individuals involved in this medium are themselves artists and scientists. Alvy Ray Smith, Dan Sandin, and A. Michael Noll were all trained in the sciences, but each have impressive art exhibition records. Larry Cuba, Chuck Csuri, and Vibeke Sorensen were all trained in the arts; however, they also obtained technical training.

Some of these individuals have had more subtle influences. James Blinn and John Whitney, Jr. were products of families where both parents were artists. Although neither have had formal art training, the aesthetic sensibility their individual work displays is obviously art-influenced.

The marriage between science and art perhaps begins with the shared desire to communicate. As Bob Hendricks of the Johns Hopkins Applied Physics Lab asserted at the 1988 SIGGRAPH conference panel:

I think that the convergence or commonality between art and science—
we have a long history of that, even *Gray's Anatomy*—the whole idea of
art and science, they have something in common. At their best, they're
supposed to be trying to convey truth. And they've always been combined
or interdependent in some ways. (1988, 15)

However, the relationship reaches beyond a shared objective, to interdependence. The artists need the technology developed by the scientists and the scientists need the visualization abilities of the artists.
SIGGRAPH chair Kellogg Booth confirms this observation:

I expect that there will always be a collaboration between scientists and
artists in this field, because scientists need the artistic insight to do their
work. (personal interview, 1 August 1988)

Artist Ed Emshwiller argued the artist's view:

I think what is needed is scientists working with artists to develop tools
which will enable us to do more and better the things we can already
do and maybe the things we can't at this point. (personal interview, 14
January 1988)

As a result, the artists influence the direction of technological development. Commercial artistic director Richard Taylor posits:

I think that in most visual forms of communication that the artists are
the ones who push the technology the furthest. That's part of what an
artist does. (personal interview, 2 August 1988)

This interdependence is also the result of the way in which the
medium evolved. Much like photography and film, computer animation pioneers were scientists, and fortunately, once again paralleling
film and photography, many such as John Whitney, Sr. and A. Michael Noll were also artists. Richard Taylor explains:

It [computer animation] started as a technical process first, and not as an
aesthetic process, and then it evolved as a result of artistic people trying
to make things happen with it. (personal interview, 2 August 1988)

Communication is an imperative issue in this medium on many
levels, beginning with a clear dialogue between the artists and the
scientists. The artists must have the ability to articulate precise needs

and the scientists must be able to express their objectives. Carl Rosendahl, founder and president of PDI, elaborates:

> You need very skilled software people who are writing the tools, and the tools are going to be used by artists. There has to be a very clean path of communication between those people. So the ideal is, rather than having a hard technician and an artist talking to each other, those people themselves overlap. So you have a technician who's got an artistic ability and an artist who's got a technical competence and that helps form the bridge that allows them to communicate and for them to support each other. (personal interview, 21 December 1988)

Another communication issue focuses on the natural evolution which any new medium experiences. Computer animation is in the early stages of establishing its own forms of communication. It has been dependent on graphics, video, photography, film, and painting for its images, even for its language. This is changing as it's developing its own form of storytelling. Carl Rosendahl explains:

> If you look at any medium for communicating, be it film, traditional animation, novels, painting, photography—there's an evolution it goes through in creating its own language, its own form of communication. (1988, 4)

Computer animation offers unlimited potential for communication. It is a powerful medium which has the ability to visualize the unseen, create environments, illustrate concepts, convey messages, and evoke emotions. It is a developing instrument which is active in the process of defining its role as an art form and communication vehicle.

"Making the invisible, visible" (Robert Abel, telephone interview, 9 May 1988) is the current driving force behind computer animation. This intent transcends disciplines and is exemplified in the visualization of scientific and mathematical data, and the communication of ideas, concepts, and theories. This is clearly evident by its emerging presence in the classrooms of universities and high schools to aid students in the visualization and comprehension of four-dimensional geometric shapes, molecule structures, physical theories, and artistic statements. Because it is losing its novelty and mystique and becoming more accessible, computer animation is moving toward becoming a more common tool. Robert Abel asserts:

> I think it [computer animation] may become as common a tool as sketching or drawing. I think it's going to become a standard tool of expression

in the same way alphabets became, or hieroglyphics. I think it's empowering people to communicate. It's a form of expression. (telephone interview, 9 May 1988)

The increased accessibility is the product of what appears to be a shared goal between software and hardware companies: to make computer animation equipment more affordable. This affordability enhances not only the usage, but the types of applications which employ computer animation. Therefore, computer animation has transcended the research laboratory and high-end production facilities to the high school classroom and the studio artist. As applications increase, so will the user community. Throughout its short history, computer animation has maintained a consistent objective to communicate. That which it has sought to communicate has been a combination of the social needs of the time and the available technology. The objective however, remains the same, to communicate.

References

Books

Chell, D. 1985. *Moviemakers at work*. New York: Microsoft Press.

Fox, D., and M. Waitz. 1984. *Computer animation primer*. New York: McGraw-Hill Book Company.

Fetter, W. 1964. *Computer graphics in communication*. New York: McGraw-Hill Book Company.

Goodman, C. 1987. *Digital visions*. New York: Henry N. Abrams, Inc., Publishers.

Halas, J., and R. Manvell. 1970. *Art in movement*. New York: Hastings House.

Jankel, A., and R. Morton. 1984. *Creative computer graphics*. Cambridge: Cambridge University Press.

Littlejohn, S. 1983. *Theories of Communication*. Belmont, Calif.: Wadsworth Publishing Company.

Madsen, R. 1969. *Animated Film: concepts, methods, uses*. New York: Interland Publishing, Inc.

Peitgen, H. 1986. *The beauty of fractals*. Berlin: Springer-Verlag.

Peterson, I. 1988. *The mathematical tourist*. New York: W. H. Freeman and Company.

Prueitt, M. 1975. *ComputerGraphics*. New York: Dover.

Prueitt, M. 1984. *Art and the computer*. New York: McGraw-Hill Book Company.

Russett, R., and C. Starr. 1976. *Experimental animation*. New York: Van Nostrand Reinhold Company.

Stephenson, R. 1973. *The animated film*. London: Tantivy Press.

Thalmann, N., and D. Thalmann. 1985. *Computer animation theory and practice*. Tokyo: Springer-Verlag.

Tucker, W. 1981. *Research in speech communication*. Englewood Cliffs, N.J.: Prentice Hall, Inc.

Whitney, J. 1980. *Digital Harmony*. Peterborough, N.H.: Byte Books.

Wilson, S. 1986. *Using computers to create art*. Englewood Cliffs, N.J.: Prentice-Hall, Inc.

Youngblood, G. 1979. *Expanded cinema*. New York: E. P. Dutton.

Interviews

Abel, Robert. Telephone interview with author. May 1988.

Banchoff, T. Interview with author; Atlanta, Georgia. August 1988.

Blinn, James. Interview with author; Pasadena, California. December 1987.

Booth, Kellogg. Interview with author; Atlanta, Georgia. August 1988.

Carpenter, Loren. Interview with author; San Rafael, California. January 1988.

Catmull, Edwin. Interview with author; San Rafael, California. May 1988.

Collery, Michael. Interview with author; Sunnyvale, California. May 1988.

Crow, Frank. Interview with author; Menlo Park, California. May 1988.

Csuri, Charles. Interview with author; Columbus, Ohio. November 1987.

Cuba, Larry. Interview with author; Santa Cruz, California. January 1988.

DeFanti, Thomas. Interview with author; Chicago, Illinois. February 1988.

Demos, Gary. Interview with author; Century City, California. May 1988.

Dietrich, Frank. Interview with author; Mountain View, California. January 1988.

Emshwiller, Ed. Interview with author; Valencia, California. January 1988.

Holzman, Robert. Interview with author; Washington, D.C. June 1988.

Katz, Louis. Interview with author; Oakland, California. May 1988.

Knowlton, Kenneth. Telephone interview with author. March 1989.

Kovacs, William. Interview with author; Santa Barbara, California. January 1988.

Kristoff, James. Interview with author; Hollywood, California. January 1988.

Lasseter, John. Interview with author; San Rafael, California. May 1988.

Ledeen, Louise Etra. Interview with author; Oakland, California. January 1988.

Max, Nelson. Interview with author; Atlanta, Georgia. August 1988.

Michael, George. Interview with author; Atlanta, Georgia. August 1988.

Mittelman, Phillip. Interview with author; Westwood, California. May 1988.

Noll, A. Michael. Interview with author; Los Angeles, California. May 1988.

Pietgen, Heinz-Otto. Interview with author; Atlanta, Georgia. August 1988.

Pepke, Eric. Interview with author; Tallahassee, Florida. March 1992.

Prince, Patric. Interview with author; Pasadena, California. January 1988.

Randall, Randy. Interview with author; Glendale, California. January 1988.

Rosebush, Judson. Interview with author; Atlanta, Georgia. August 1988.

Rosendahl, Carl. Interview with author; Sunnyvale, California. December 1988.

Sandin, Daniel. Interview with author; Chicago, Illinois. February 1988.

Smith, Alvy Ray. Interview with author; San Rafael, California. May 1988.

Sorensen, Vibeke. Interview with author; Valencia, California. January 1988.

Taylor, Richard. Interview with author; Atlanta, Georgia. August 1988.

Veeder, Jane. Interview with author; Santa Barbara, California. January 1988.

Wein, Marceli. Interview with author; Atlanta, Georgia. August 1988.

Whitney, John Jr. Interview with author; Century City, California. May 1988.

Whitney, John Sr. Interview with author; Palos Verdes, California. December 1987.

Whitted, Turner. Interviewed with author; Atlanta, Georgia. August 1988.

Periodicals

Mancis A., and W. Van Dyke. 1966. "Artist as Filmmaker." *Art in America*: 54, 100.

Noll, A. Michael "Computer generated three-dimensional movies." *Computers and Automation*.

Smith, A. October 1982. "Special effects for Star Trek II." *American Cinematographer*: 1038–1039; 1048; 1050.

O'Neill, J. March/April 1986. "Exploring the mechanical universe with computer graphics." *Computer Pictures*: 30–35.

Smith, A. "Digital filmmaking." *ABACUS*: 28–45.

Van Dam, A. 1984. "Computer software for graphics." *Scientific American*: 158.

Wilson, M. 1986. "History of computer graphics and computer animation in the United States through 1985." *Animation*: 12–28.

Dissertations

Sutherland, I. 1963. "Sketchpad: a man-machine graphical communication system" (Ph.D. diss., MIT, 1963).

Conference Proceedings

Crow, F. 1977. "The aliasing problem in computer-generated shaded images." *Communications of the ACM* 20: 799–805.

Hendricks, R. 1988. "Computer graphics, and the changing methodology for artists and designers." *Proceedings Siggraph '88*: 1–22.

Kajiya, J. 1983. "New Techniques for ray tracing procedurally defined objects." *Proceedings Siggraph '82, Computer Graphics,* 16 (3): 245–254.

Kaprow, A. 1988. "Computer graphics and the changing methodology for artist and designers." *Proceedings Siggraph '88:* 1–22.

Knowlton, K. 1968. "Computer animated movies." *Cybernetic Serendipity, a special issue of Studio International,* Ed. Jasia Reichardt (London, September, 1968): 67–68.

Lanthrop, O. 1988. "Fundamentals and overview of computer graphics." *Association For Computing Machinery's Special Interest Group on Computer Graphics 15th Annual Conference Course Notes.* pp. IV 1–IV 28.

Machover, C. 1988. "Fundamentals and overview of computer graphics." *Association For Computing Machinery's Special Interest Grow on Computer Graphics 15th Annual Conference Course Notes.* pp. V 1–V 366.

Parke, F. 1972. "Animation of faces." *Proceedings ACM Annual Conference,* 1.

Rosebush, J. 1988. "Introduction to computer animation." *Association For Computing Machinery's Special Interest Group on Computer Graphics 15th Annual Conference Course Notes.*

Rosebush, J. 1980. "Computer animation: An historical survey." In 1980 National Computer Graphics Association Conference Proceedings.

Slayton, J. 1980. "Computer graphics and the changing methodology for artist and designers." *Proceedings Siggraph '88:* 1–22.

Newspaper Articles

Perlman, M. 9 October 1980. "The artist and the computer." *Santa Barbara News and Review.*

Solomon, C. 2 November 1983. "Computer: soaring with animation." *Los Angeles Times:* 1, 6.

Technical Memos

Smith, A. 1978. *Paint.* Technical Memo No. 7.

Other Works Cited

Armbrust, R. 1983, January/February. "The simulation of space." *Computer Pictures:* 24–27.

Blinn, J. 1977. "Models of light reflection for computer synthesized pictures." *Proceedings Siggraph 1977* 11: 192–98.

Blinn, J. 1978. Computer display of curved surfaces. (Doctoral dissertation, University of Utah).

Blinn, J. 1978. "Simulation of wrinkled surfaces." *Proceedings Siggraph 1978* 12: 286–92.

Blinn, J. 1982. "Light reflections for simulation of clouds and dusty surfaces." *Proceedings Siggraph 1982* 16: 21–29.

Booth, S., D. H. Kochanek, M. Wein. 1983. "Computers animate film and video." *IEEE Spectrum:* 44–51.

J. Borrell 1981. "The magic of computer animation." *Computer Graphics World:* 25–33.

Burtnyk, N., J. K. Pulfer, M. Wein. 1971. Computer graphics and film animation. *INFUR:* 1–11.

Burtnyk, N. and M. Wein. 1971. "Computer generated Key-frame animation." *Journal of Society for Motion Picture and Television Engineers* 80: 149–53.

Burtnyk, N. & M. Wein. 1971. "A computer animation system for the animator." *Proceedings UAIDE 10th Annual Meeting:* 3–24.

Catmull, E. 1972. "A system for computer generated movies." *Proceedings ACM Annual Conference:* 422–431.

Catmull, E. 1978. "The problem of computer-assisted animation." *Computer Graphics,* 12: 348–353.

Catmull, E. 1978. "A hidden-surface algorithm with anti-aliasing." *Proceedings Siggraph,* 12: 6–11.

Crow, F. C. 1977. "The aliasing problem in computer-generated shaded images." *Communications of the ACM* 20: 799–805.

Crow, F. C. 1977. "Shadow algorithms for computer graphics." *Proceedings Siggraph 1977* 11, 242–248.

Crow, F. C. 1978. "Shaded computer graphics in the entertainment industry." *Computer, IEEE Press* 11: 11–23.

Crow. F. C. 1981. "A comparison of anti-aliasing techniques." *IEEE Computer Graphics and Applications* 1: 40–48.

Csuri, C. 1970. "Real-time film animation." *Proceedings 9th UAIDE Annual Meeting:* 289–305.

Csuri, C. 1974. "Real-time computer animation." *Proceedings IFIP Congress 1974:* 707–711.

Csuri, C. 1974. "Computer graphics and art." *Proceedings IEEE* 62: 503–515.

Csuri, C. 1975. "Computer animation." *Proceedings Siggraph 1975* 9: 92–101.

DeFanti, T. 1976. "The digital component of the circle graphics habitat." *Proceedings National Computer Conference* 1976: 195–203.

DeFanti, T. & D. Sandin. 1987. "The usable intersection of pc graphics and NTSC video recording." *IEEE Computer Graphics and Applications:* 50–58.

DeFanti, T. 1988, January/February. "Cultural roadblocks to visualization." *Computers in Science:* 4–6.

Ex-CCP President Jim Kristoff launches North Light Studios in L.A. (1987, October). *Back Stage* 4–5.

Fetter, W. A. 1982. "A Progression of human figures simulated by computer graphics." *IEEE Computer Graphics and Applications* 2: 9–13.

Friesen, D. P. 1969. "A professional animator looks at computer animation." *Proceedings 8th UAIDE Annual Meeting:* 187–94.

Goss, T. 1983, March/April. "Animation and the new machine." *Print:* 57–64.

Hadley, C. 9 October 1987. "Columbus' Cranston-Csuri files for chapter 11; high overhead blamed." *Back Stage:* 1, 47.

Hadley, C. 16 October 1987. Questions remain unanswered in wake of Cranston-Csuri closing. *Back Stage:* 7, 45.

Honey, F. J. 1971. "Artist oriented computer animation." *Journal of Society of Motion Pictures and Television Engineers,* 80, 154.

Kajiya, J. T. 1982. "Ray tracing parametric patches." *Proceedings Siggraph 1982* 16: 245–254.

Kajiya, J. T. 1983. "New techniques for ray tracing procedurally defined objects." *Proceedings Siggraph 1983* 17: 91–99.

Kallis, S. A. 1971. "Computer animation techniques." *Journal of the SMPTE* 80: 145–148.

Knowlton, K. C. 1964. "A computer technique for producing animated movies." *Proceedings AFIPS Conference* 25: 67–87.

Knowlton, K. C. 1965. "Computer-produced movies." *Science:* 150, 1116–1120.

Knowlton, K. C. 1972. "Collaboration with artist: a programmer's reflections." *Proceedings IFIP:* 399–418.

Levine, S. R. 1975. "Computer animation at Lawrence Livermore Laboratory." *Proceedings Siggraph 1975* 9: 81–84.

Lewell, J. 1981, October. "The computer paintings of David Em." *Business Screen:* 38–40.

Lewell, J. 1983. "The pioneers: John Whitney Sr." *Computer Pictures* 1: 22–24.

Magnenat-Thalmann, N., A. Larouche A., & D. Thalmann. 1983. "An interactive and user-oriented three-dimensional graphics editor." *Proceedings Graphics Interface 1983:* 39–46.

Magnenat-Thalmann, N. & D. Thalmann. 1983. The use of 3-D high-level graphical types in the MIRA animation system." *IEEE Computer Graphics and Application* 3: 9–16.

Mandlebrot, B. B. 1977. *Fractals: form, chance and dimension.* San Francisco: Freeman.

Mandlebrot, B. B. 1982. *The fractal geometry of nature.* San Francisco: Freeman.

Mittelman, P. 1983. "Computer graphics at MAGI." Proceedings 1983 Online Conference: 291–301.

Negroponte, N. 1976. "Experiments with computer animation." *Computer Graphics,* 10: 40–44.

Noll, A. M. 1965. "Stereographic projections by digital computers." *Computers and Automation* 14: 32–34.

Noll, A. M. 1965, November. "Computer generated three-dimensional movies." *Computers and Application,* 20.

Noll, A. M. 1967. "Computers and the visual arts." *Design and Planning* 2: 65–80.

Noll, A. M. 1968. "Computer animation and the fourth dimension." *Proceedings AFIPS Conference* 33: 1279–1283.

Reeves, W. T. 1981. "In-betweening for computer animation utilizing moving point constraints." *Proceedings Siggraph 1981* 15: 263–269.

Rubin, S. & Whitted, T. 1980. "A three-dimensional representation for fast rendering of complex scenes." *Proceedings Siggraph 1980* 14: 110–116.

Shoup, R. G. 1979, May. "Superpaint: the digital animator." *Dramation:* 150–156.

Wein, M. & Burtnyk, N. 1972. "A computer facility for film animation and music." *Proceedings CIPS 1972:* 201–212.

Zajac, E. E. 1965. "Computer animation a new scientific and educational tool." *SMPTE* 74: 1006–1008.

Zajac, E. E. 1966. "Film animation by computer." *New Scientist,* 29: 346–349.

Books

Fetter, W. A. 1964. *Computer graphics in communication.* New York: McGraw-Hill Book Company.

Halas, J. & R. Manvell. 1968. *The technique of film animation.* New York: Hastings House.

Halas, J. 1974. *Computer animation.* New York: Hastings House.

Levitan, E. L. 1977. *Electronic imaging techniques.* New York: Van Nostrand.

Index